Praise for *Destination Profit*

"Illuminates and helps guide readers along a path to business success that has been underexplored for too long: the very real connection between making money and creating a work environment that values people."

—DONNA FREY, LEADER OF HUMAN RESOURCES,
W. L. GORE & ASSOCIATES, INC.

"An insightful examination of how forward-thinking companies create a great place to work. Learn how revolutionary leaders improve profitability while keeping morale high and turnover low through decisions that create a performance-driven culture. A must-read for managers who want to have a positive impact on their organization."

—DARRIN EMERICK, CHIEF PERSONNEL OFFICER,
PERKINS COIE LLP

"The first application-based guide designed to help CEOs realize the value of their greatest asset—people—by inspiring them to build a corporate culture that embraces and champions performance greatness to drive profitability."

—JET PARKER, CHIEF VISIONARY OFFICER, CEO IQ

"*Today, the only way to deliver what a customer needs is to first focus on your employees. Cawood and Bailey show the reader 1001 ways that 'People = Profit.' Organizations that take employees for granted will be left in the dust by their competitors.*"

"*The authors have done a phenomenal job of getting to the real issues related to sustaining a successful organization through your people. The message is so simple it is remarkable. An excellent resource for any organization that is committed to moving to new heights..*"

"*The authors have hit the nail on the head. The key to outstanding financial performance lies in people—their performance, their motivation, and their engagement. A great read.*"

Destination Profit

destination profit

Creating People-Profit Opportunities in Your Organization

SCOTT CAWOOD

RITA V. BAILEY

DAVIES-BLACK PUBLISHING
Mountain View, California

Published by Davies-Black Publishing, a division of CPP, Inc., 1055 Joaquin Road, 2nd Floor, Mountain View, CA 94043; 800-624-1765.

Special discounts on bulk quantities of Davies-Black books are available to corporations, professional associations, and other organizations. For details, contact the Director of Marketing and Sales at Davies-Black Publishing: 650-691-9123; fax 650-623-9271.

Davies-Black and its colophon are registered trademarks of CPP, Inc.

Visit the Davies-Black Publishing Web site at www.daviesblack.com.

10 09 08 07 06   10 9 8 7 6 5 4 3 2 1

Printed in the United States of America

Library of Congress Cataloging-in-Publication Data

Cawood, Scott.
    Destination profit: creating people-profit opportunities in your organization /
    Scott Cawood and Rita V. Bailey.—1st ed.
        p. cm.
    Includes bibliographical references and index.
    ISBN-13: 978-0-89106-196-0 (hardcover)
    ISBN-10: 0-89106-196-7 (hardcover)
    1. Employee empowerment. 2. Organizational effectiveness. I. Bailey, Rita V.
    (Rita Vancil). II. Title.
    HD50.5.C39 2006
    658.3'14—dc22

                                2006009840

FIRST EDITION
First printing 2006

To my mother, Georgia Cawood, with much gratitude and love
—SCOTT CAWOOD

To my mother, Annie M. Alexander, for her unwavering faith, encouragement, and love
—RITA BAILEY

CONTENTS

Preface *xi*

Acknowledgments *xvii*

About the Authors *xxi*

1 The People Connection
Seeking Organizations That Do It 1

2 Pathways to Profitability
Finding a New Way 33

3 The 4-A Process
A Tool for Maximizing Business Growth 89

4 Awareness
Planning Your Destination 111

5 **Alignment**
Charting the Course to Your Destination 139

6 **Accountability**
Empowering through a Shared Purpose 161

7 **Adaptation**
Evolving Every Day 181

8 **The Human Side**
Focusing on the Enduring Thing 211

Notes *231*

Index *233*

PREFACE

Enough, already, of complex management theories! Building your bottom line is a simple equation: Engaged People = Enriched Profits. The best way to survive, compete, or thrive in any type of economy is through the experience you provide for your employees—one that will fully connect them to your organization and drive business toward you.

A Walk around the Block

When the two of us first met in 2000 at a conference in San Francisco, our connection was immediate. We spontaneously took a walk around the block—actually, several city blocks—and began sharing our ideas. At that time, we both worked at outstanding companies recognized as highly profitable and great places to work—Rita at Southwest Airlines and Scott at W. L. Gore & Associates. As we traded stories of our positive, often incredible, work experiences, we discovered we shared a passion for getting the word out on what we've found to be true: When companies provide their people with an engaging work experience, they make a lot more money.

The more we walked, the more we talked. The more we talked, the clearer it all seemed. On the one hand, companies become more profitable by intentionally connecting with their people and by connecting their people with one another, with their jobs, and with what we call the Optimum People-Profit Opportunities, or OPPOs, of their organizations. People stay. Profits flow. Organizations grow. On the other hand, those who can't engage their people lose employees. Lose money. And often become another illustration of what not to do that ends up studied in an MBA program.

Southwest Airlines and JetBlue Airways are good examples of the impact that strong people relations can have on profits, especially in times of crisis. Both companies have managed to maintain profitability despite the turbulence their industry has faced—the unprecedented terrorist attacks of 9/11 and the economic slowdown that followed, a dramatic downturn in business travel, an outbreak of Severe Acute Respiratory Syndrome (SARS), international conflicts, soaring fuel prices, and bankruptcies. While the industry lost more than $35 billion between 2001 and 2005—more than it made in the past 50 years—Southwest and JetBlue have maintained their profitability. Their emphasis on building people-centric cultures has been the prime factor in driving profit.

As is true for most industries, there are more challenging times ahead for the airlines, but they have responded to tough times before and are well positioned to do so again because of their people. In 2006, there is no doubt that JetBlue will face a tough year. Rising fuel costs, higher-than-expected operating costs, and rapid expansion plans present even more challenges for the airline. We believe, however, that JetBlue is positioned as best it can be to work through these issues because, like Southwest, it realizes the power of people.

Why is this link between people and profits so obvious, yet so difficult for most organizations to make? From that question alone, a series of spirited conversations cascaded between the two of us. Four years of conversations, in fact. And then, thought by thought, and interview by interview, we mined this book.

During this time, we both became independent advisers, helping organizations understand the principles and practices associated with developing people cultures. Our passion comes from having "been there and done that"—gaining firsthand experience inside highly successful organizations. In writing this book, we were driven by the pressing need to speak to people's desire for meaning and purpose and to engage with organizations that have great people but may lack the processes and interactions that will truly connect these employees to the business.

Reality Check

Is your business plan the same as those of your competitors? How about your mission statement and strategic priorities? Whose products or services will become obsolete first, yours or theirs? In what area can you really compete, surge ahead, and dominate? We believe the experience you create for your people is the real competitive advantage.

Other books on workforce productivity have focused on how to improve things—streamlining operations, enhancing technology, or planning more strategically. But, no matter how you look at it, people make business happen. When you don't have a culture that connects people to your business, fosters innovation, and encourages communication, it's not long before systems break down. Work teams disconnect, productivity declines, and profits sag.

Employees always have the choice of simply showing up each day at work, doing just enough to get by, and only looking forward to Fridays. Some, however, do more than just show up. They participate in the business and give the organization what it needs to execute on goals and strategies. The defining difference between these two types of employees is not their skill set, motivation to work, or even desire to get a paycheck. The difference is whether they feel connected to their organizations and have meaningful reasons to perform.

We have found that people who are treated as if they can make a difference usually do. They will come to work and care about their jobs, their colleagues, and their organizations. They will give more than they have to, take ownership of the business, and produce dynamic results. Unlike those who just show up for the paychecks, these engaged employees will lead their organizations to profitability.

Take a walk around your organization. What's really going on? What's the typical experience of an average employee on an average day? Do your people enjoy coming to work? Are they truly living your company's values? Do they like what they're doing? Are they driving business toward you, or away?

Wherever you are in the process of linking people with profits, this book of strategies and stories can help you get there. Throughout, you'll find real-world insights from CEOs, executives, and even line managers who are doing it today. We've found that organizations can be divided into two camps: Those whose employees say, "Why should we?" and those whose employees say, "How can we?" What do your employees say?

The organizations we highlight here are all "how can we" organizations—paradigm breakers that have dared to be different. Some are included in *Fortune*'s 100 Best Companies to Work For, but just as many are not. Some are huge organizations; some are small. Some are privately held, others are public, and some are nonprofit. They also represent a variety of industries, from transportation to health care, manufacturing to information technology. What they share is the drive to create a workplace where people want to work and where that commitment drives profit.

Most of the concepts in this book may seem simple, but they are not necessarily easy. There's a huge difference between knowing what to do and being able to do it. We have studied many successful organizations that have done it: They all started with the mind-set that investing in people yields high returns.

The 4-A Process

To help you develop a People = Profits point of view, we've included the 4-A Process, which is designed to help you think your way into acting differently, in new ways that will revolutionize your thinking. Increase awareness of your Destination. Align every part of your organization through shared goals. Use accountability to transform your goals into actions. And make small adjustments that will help you adapt along the way.

Here's what the chapter line-up looks like: Chapter 1 introduces 13 exemplary organizations that keep the concept of Engaged People = Enriched Profits constantly at the forefront of doing business. Chapter 2 focuses on the seven Pathways to Profitability taken by these and other companies, and chapter 3 gives an overview of the 4-A Process. Chapters 4 through 7 feature each of the 4-As—Awareness, Alignment, Accountability, and

Adaptation—in depth. Chapter 8 emphasizes the all-important communication and celebration aspects of business that are too often forgotten. Throughout, you'll see focus questions and exercises designed to help you apply our ideas to your organization's teams as well as its individuals.

Take a walk with us! Whether you're just starting out, have been around for a while, or are ready for a makeover, the information in this book can help you become a higher-performing organization. Begin the journey toward your Destination of greatness now! Welcome aboard.

ACKNOWLEDGMENTS

This part of the book will be easiest for me to write, as I genuinely and unequivocally remain in gratitude to the following:

Christopher Bramfitt, for your extraordinary contribution to every part of this book and my life; Rita Bailey, for following this dream with me; Sue Carrington, for your excellence in writing and your unwavering dedication to this book—which would not have been done without you.

Rich Boyer, whose skill, energy, and passion help to ignite change, and Eileen Edmunds, Susan Needham, and Rebecca Billingsley, who continue to lead the way at ModernThink. We have taken on the challenge of changing how the world works, one organization at a time!

All contributors to this book, especially Terry Andrus of East Alabama Medical Center, Captain Mike Barger of JetBlue Airlines, Cathy Benton of Alston & Bird, Jeff Chambers of SAS Institute, Darrin Emerick of Perkins Coie, Terri Kelly of W. L. Gore & Associates, and Kelly Semrau of SC Johnson. I am inspired by your stories and honored that you would give so willingly to this book; thank you!

W. L. Gore & Associates, especially Sally Gore, Susan Dill, Donna Frey, Sonia Dunbar, Heidi Cofran, Josh Selekman, Vicki Cotter, and Gail Townsend—you all helped me more than I will ever be able to acknowledge here. To Ms. Carol Burnett for your faith in all things good, and a very special thanks to everyone who worked with me at the Barksdale plant. It was the best job I ever had!

Regan MacBain-Traub, who continues to inspire us all to make it count; Linda Rappaport, whose energy and wisdom have opened doors to so many; and Linda Mattia-Potts, who through such adversity has risen to the challenges time and time again: to each of you, I am truly indebted.

Brian Lange for your continued friendship, generosity, and counsel, and Georgia Jacobs, who constantly inspired me to write.

Connie Kallback and Laura Simonds of Davies-Black Publishing; you are both exceptional at what you do.

Carol and Greg Perry, Donna Cawood, Joy Barrett, and Randy and Patti Cawood, I appreciate all you have done to contribute to my life and my work—in case it went without saying, I am proud to call you my family.

—Scott Cawood

The experience of writing this book was a bit like riding a roller-coaster—at times thrilling and exhilarating and sometimes frightening and stressful. When the ride is over there's a sense of relief, accomplishment, and confidence. The best part is celebrating with the people who took the ride with you.

My sincere appreciation goes to all the people who gave unselfishly of their time, resources, and support: Scott for the wonderful experience of coauthoring this book with you. Connie, Laura, and the team at Davies-Black for providing guidance and encouragement throughout the process. ASTD for co-publishing, and especially Tony, Cat, Pat, and the entire team for being our biggest fan club. Sue Carrington, our writing partner, who burned the midnight oil many nights to help us weave together thoughts, stories, and interviews. Pat Jannausch of Conway, Sunny Vanderbeck and Rand Stagen of Data Return, and the Southwest Airlines family for sharing model practices that exemplify great workplaces and people cultures.

Thank you to the many friends, colleagues, and family members who were there to provide support, resources, and encouragement. Charmione, thanks for your dedication to doing whatever was necessary to get the job done. Henry, you are my rock. Thanks for helping me stay focused, providing insight and perspective, and being there through every stage of the process, and for your unconditional love and support.

—Rita Bailey

ABOUT THE AUTHORS

Scott Cawood, Ph.D., SPHR, is president of ModernThink, an innovative consulting firm dedicated to changing how the world works. Through his work, he partners with organizational leaders interested in building and sustaining profitable businesses where both employees and customers benefit from a people-focused workplace.

Formerly, Cawood was vice president of the Great Place to Work Institute, the firm that selects the list of "100 Best Companies to Work For in America," which appears annually in *Fortune*. He has also served as vice president for global talent management at Revlon and as a human resources leader at W. L. Gore & Associates, one of only five companies to make the "100 Best Companies" list every year since its inception.

As a recognized speaker and expert on workplace issues, Cawood has presented to audiences throughout the world on linking people and profits and is one of the Society for Human Resource Management's (SHRM) "Top Ten" speakers. He holds a Ph.D. degree in business and organizational behavior. Cawood can be contacted at scawood@modernthink.com

Rita V. Bailey is founder and CEO of QVF Partners, Ltd., where she works with organizations, entrepreneurs, and leaders to develop values-based, people-driven cultures that yield high-performance results. She has worked in various industries including transportation, service, technology, and health care.

Prior to starting her own company, Bailey served in several leadership positions during her 25-year career at Southwest Airlines in such varied areas as customer service, marketing, public relations, and human resources. She headed Southwest Airlines' University for People, in which capacity she was responsible for the design, development, and implementation of leadership and personal development programs.

She also helped develop and implement the Advanced Leadership: High Potential, High Performance Program at SMU Cox School of Business Executive Education.

Bailey is a well-known expert, speaker, and advisor on topics including organizational culture, people strategies, leadership, service, and innovation. She has presented to and worked with groups in Europe, Mexico, Brazil, Australia, and Asia. As 2005 chair of the American Society for Training and Development (ASTD) she has spoken to chapters worldwide on topics related to learning strategies. She can be contacted at rita@qvfpartners.com.

(1) THE PEOPLE CONNECTION

Seeking Organizations That Do It

We're living in a time when competition is more grueling than ever, customers are far less forgiving, we all have to do more with less—and do it faster, often in a virtual environment. When we add the global and economic implications of doing business today, it's no wonder that many organizations struggle to take off or reach their intended Destinations. Organizations that can't adapt and learn to compete will find themselves irrelevant and, eventually, extinct. We don't want to scare you into action, but we do want to equip you with enough information to be formidable!

What will distinguish your organization from the rest? You guessed it: your people. Regardless of whether you deliver a service, make a product, or provide information, your people will

1

make the difference in how fast, and how fruitfully, your business grows. At a time when one company can look pretty much like another, we believe the only true competitive advantage today is the experience you provide your people—an experience that is so compelling, and so connective, that the deliverables they return to you and your customers enable you to outperform your competition.

In the People Business

We overheard a speaker at a major conference suggest that when managers have to make hard decisions, it's "business, not personal." What was he thinking? In *Competing for Talent,* Nancy Ahlrichs makes it clear: Everything that happens to people inside an organization is personal, not business. "It's all personal," she says.[1] And she's right. For example, when a company decides to lay off part of its workforce for business reasons, there is definitely a personal effect. Even those who remain are personally affected when colleagues leave.

Sure, we have different products and industries, but a common misstep among leaders is to think that it's somehow a smart business strategy to separate business and people. Jack Welch, former CEO of General Electric, said it best when he quipped, "If you aren't teaching and coaching, you aren't leading."

Smart leaders understand that all businesses are in the people business, and the actual product or service is simply an output—something that others can make or do but that seems different only because of who makes it or how it is delivered. They work hard to leverage the potential that exists at the organizational, team, and individual levels.

This philosophy, that all businesses are in the people business, is one that W. L. Gore & Associates, makers of the popular

GORE-TEX® fabric, has followed since its start in 1958. Founder Wilbert (Bill) Gore and his wife, Genevieve (Vieve), understood just how critical a culture is to business success. In fact, they defined the culture of Gore as a people business even before they had a product to sell! Over the years, Gore's culture—phenomenal people, passionate about what they're doing and committed to building exceptional teams—has skyrocketed the company to annual revenue of $1.8 billion.

> *"You can't separate culture*
> *and business results. The link*
> *is what makes it work."*

—Terri Kelly, CEO, W. L. Gore & Associates, Inc.

Bob Doak, a leader in one of Gore's divisions, suggests that Gore associates are some of the most connected to any business, anywhere. Everyone at Gore understands that the company's Optimum People-Profit Opportunity is the application of the polymer polytetrafluoroethylene (PTFE) and strives every day on the job to find new ways to use it. This connection to the business has resulted in Gore being named the most innovative company on the planet and one of the best places in the world to work, according to *Fortune*.[2] More important to Gore than external validation, however, is the internal vote of confidence, as reflected in its tremendously low turnover rates and the discretionary effort its associates consistently offer.

Terri Kelly, CEO, notes that Gore's customers feel the impact of the company's culture, too. "Our best validation is when our customers experience the difference. We often hear that they feel a level of commitment and excitement from our associates that they don't feel with other suppliers," she notes.

PEOPLE = PROFIT: PROOF THAT IT WORKS

W. L. Gore & Associates began in Newark, Delaware, in 1958, when Bill and Vieve Gore set out to explore opportunities for fluorocarbon polymers. Within the first 12 years, Gore had operations worldwide. Today, the enterprise includes about 7,000 associates in 45 locations around the world and annual revenues of more than $1.8 billion. Although best known for its GORE-TEX® fabric, the company provides innovative solutions to many industries, from electronics to medicine. Gore has repeatedly been named among *Fortune*'s 100 Best Companies to Work For in America.

Southwest Airlines has an open culture that encourages its people to envision the impossible, share their thoughts, and challenge the status quo. That kind of freedom to be real connects people to the bigger picture of what their business is all about. Imagine that connection—multiplied by 33,000 employees!

With values that include words like *family, fun, love, individuality, ownership, altruism,* and *egalitarianism,* it's no wonder Southwest employees feel connected. You see these values in action when a flight attendant sings the announcements or when employees go out of their way to assist a customer or co-worker or to pitch in on a community project.

Southwest employees are confident that the company will support them in almost every situation if their intention is to "do the right thing." Mistakes are forgiven, risk-taking is encouraged, and fun and celebration are an everyday occurrence. Southwest receives more than 200,000 applications and résumés every year—an indication, in the depressed airline industry, that they must be doing a lot of things right.

PEOPLE = PROFIT: PROOF THAT IT WORKS

Southwest Airlines, headquartered in Dallas, Texas, has more than 31,000 employees throughout the country. The airline began service in June 1971, with flights between Houston, Dallas, and San Antonio. Today, it flies nearly 3,000 flights a day to 62 cities in 32 states. With 34 consecutive years of profitability, Southwest is the most successful low-fare, high-frequency, point-to-point carrier in the United States. Southwest has always considered itself a customer service organization that happens to be an airline.

SAS Institute (SAS), the world's largest privately held software maker, is renowned for its people practices. When company founder Jim Goodnight started SAS in 1976, he wanted to build a different type of organization, a place where people could be empowered. He believed people were the best investment he could make in his business, because satisfied employees create satisfied customers.

> *"If you treat people like they*
> *make a difference, they will."*
>
> —Jim Goodnight, Founder, SAS Institute

That perspective has led to a legendary menu of employee amenities, all of which make life better for people. A 300-acre, well-manicured office campus displaying original works of art. Private offices for all professional employees. An on-site health care center and recreation and fitness center. A work-life center offering on-site daycare for 600 children, plus elder care, financial planning, teen workshops, and adoption assistance. Atrium-like cafeterias in which employees enjoy low-cost lunches and live piano music. A 35-hour workweek, with most people taking off by 5:00 p.m. Complimentary M&Ms in every break room on Wednesdays, and breakfast on Fridays. The list goes on and on.

This type of culture can sometimes breed an entitlement mentality. "People who haven't worked anywhere else don't realize how good they have it," says Jeff Chambers, SAS's vice president of human resources. "On the other hand, some people look at us and say, 'This is too weird. It's too Stepfordish. You're like a cult.'" Yet, Chambers explains that a lot of people come to work each day just to do the jobs they love and don't feel the need to take advantage of the amenities. In the eyes of SAS, though, the perks will always be part of the value proposition of treating people as if they make a difference.

PEOPLE = PROFIT: PROOF THAT IT WORKS

SAS Institute, Inc., is a privately owned software company headquartered in Carey, North Carolina. It is a leader in e-intelligence software and services that enable customers to turn raw data into usable knowledge for better business decisions. SAS serves more than 35,000 business, government, and university sites in 110 countries. Founded in 1976, the company today has more than 9,000 employees and 295 offices worldwide. SAS has consistently been among the best companies to work for and was included six times among the top 10 of *Fortune*'s 100 Best Companies to Work For.

>> *Is the experience you provide for your people a competitive advantage? How tightly are your culture and business results linked? Do you treat your people as if they make a difference? Do your employees know they **are** the difference?*

Toward You, or Away from You?

We've worked in highly successful, profitable, people-driven companies, like Gore and Southwest, and interacted with hundreds of organizations, like SAS, whose people initiatives have spearheaded business growth. What we find over and over is this: Employees are busy doing one of two things—driving business toward their organizations or driving it away.

Think about a bad customer-service experience. We've all had them. The person you spoke with didn't seem to be happy about being there; she had trouble answering your questions about the company's products or services; when there was a problem, she didn't offer any help to fix it. Afterward, you probably weren't interested in returning as a customer.

People who give bad customer service may not lack the appropriate skills. More likely, these employees work for a company that doesn't treat them as well as it wants them to treat customers. If leaders are sending the message that they don't care about their people, their people will in turn send that message on to the world.

Now, consider an extraordinary customer-service experience. The person was enthusiastic and genuinely engaged in the interaction; he asked the right questions so that he could give you the best solution to meet your needs; he did what he could to make it right and build a long-term relationship. When you were done, not only were you likely to go back, but you probably told as many people as you could about the experience.

Picture the environment in which this enthusiastic and engaged customer-service rep works. We can only imagine that the company is providing a connective employee experience—treating employees well so that they treat customers well and can see how their individual success contributes to overall success. We can imagine, too, that this company has a culture that encourages its teams to be innovative, continually creating products and services that meet customer needs.

> > *Ask people on your team what five things they did today to (1) make deposits to the business and (2) make withdrawals from the business.*

Organizations that succeed in connecting people are finding there is no limit to their ability to drive business toward their organization—to innovate, excel, and exceed stakeholder expectations. Connected people are motivated to be more effective and results oriented. They're willing to do what it takes to see the organization succeed because they have a reason to care. Returns are reflected through such measures as superior financial performance, higher productivity, better quality at lower cost, and reduced employee turnover. If more companies connect with their people, we can surely expect connections to spread in a positive way beyond the walls of the organization. Better companies make better industries, and better industries make better societies.

> *"The only real difference is the people*
> *we attract and retain."*
>
> —Pat Jannausch, Vice President of
> Culture and Training, Con-way

Knowing that connected people drive business forward has worked well for Con-way, one of the most profitable transportation and supply chain management companies in the United States. Con-way encourages its employees to take the time to develop relationships with customers. Not only does this make the employee experience more meaningful, but it also helps build customer loyalty.

"We realized early on that any trucking company can produce the same equipment we drive and travel the same routes," says Pat Jannausch, Con-way's vice president of culture and training. "So we devote ourselves, above all else, to treating people right and building a company that they're proud to be associated with."

PEOPLE = PROFIT: PROOF THAT IT WORKS

Con-way is a $4.2 billion transportation and supply chain services company. It has earned a leadership position in its industry by providing service excellence to its customers, challenging and rewarding careers to its employees, and a superior return on shareholder investment. The company has more than 24,000 employees located in 20 countries.

>> *Do your employees sell a single product? Or do they sell an experience?*

The More Effective Bottom Line

We've seen that so many employees view their work as simply a job. They show up, do what they need to do (or less), and can't wait to get home. These people hate Mondays and Tuesdays and live for Fridays because they won't have to come to work for two days. They're an expensive and, unfortunately, all-too-familiar statistic.

A Gallup Organization study finds that almost three-quarters of employees fit this profile. They're not engaged with or are actively disengaged from their organizations—physically present on the job, but, emotionally and psychologically, they quit a long time ago. We've always thought that it's better for your employees to quit and leave than to quit and stay!

The disengaged are toxic to colleagues and customers, and they're expensive, costing U.S. businesses about $300 billion a year, the *Gallup Management Journal* says, as shown in such tangible indicators as low productivity, high turnover, reduced profits, and a waning customer base.

The effect is subtle, too. What's the cost of unhappy employees who tell their workday woes to the world? How much damage does this do to an organization's reputation and ability to attract top talent? Who wants to work at a place that has a bad rap? Who wants to buy its products or use its services?

> > *What do employees say about your workplace experience, and how does that attract or deter new customers and potential new hires?*

Over the years, Rita has become an astute observer of the airline industry and has sampled a variety of airlines beyond her alma mater, Southwest. On one flight with a legacy carrier, she stood in line waiting for the agents to open for check-in service. From the way they interacted with one another, they seemed to be friendly, happy people. But what a transformation when they started receiving customers! Their entire attitude changed, as if they were annoyed that the customers had interrupted their social time.

As Rita checked in, the agent noted that Rita worked for Southwest, and her attitude immediately changed again. For the next 10 minutes, with no regard for the other people standing in line, she proceeded to tell Rita how miserable it was to work for the company and how there was no respect or appreciation for the employees, which was why she was going to support the pending strike. She ended the conversation by saying how much she regretted not applying at Southwest first.

Beyond these kinds of face-to-face encounters, opportunities to "dish the dirt" on the employee experience are limitless, thanks to the Internet. It's no wonder many job hunters look there before pursuing potential employers. More than ever, employers need to ensure the integrity of their people experience—lest their disaster stories find a worldwide audience.

>> *Do you know what's out there on the Web about your organization?*

Accessible Leaders

They say that change flows from the top down, so it is vital that the top be visible and a part of everyday business. This isn't to say that leaders can personally get to know every individual in their organizations, but they can create an atmosphere of open communication and accessibility, sending the message that they value every person as an individual and that their doors are always open.

"If you really want to engage people in your business, you need to deal with them one-on-one."

—Joni Reich, Senior Vice President of Administration, Sallie Mae

Even though Sallie Mae, the nation's leading provider of education funding, is a large company by any standard, it strives to operate like a small business, according to Joni Reich, senior vice president of administration. "No matter how big you get—we're 10,000 employees and growing—you can't lose sight of the fact that you have to deal with individuals personally," she says. "Forgetting that is risky. That's when employees start to feel you've become arbitrary and distant, and they lose connection with what you're all about."

PEOPLE = PROFIT: PROOF THAT IT WORKS

Sallie Mae, the top U.S. company for funding college, has helped millions of Americans achieve their dream of a higher education. The company primarily provides federally guaranteed student loans and offers comprehensive information and resources to assist students, parents, and guidance professionals with the financial aid process.

Sallie Mae currently owns or manages student loans for 8 million borrowers and employs 10,000 individuals at offices nationwide. The company is listed on the Fortune 500 and the Forbes 500. It also has been recognized as one of the 100 Best Corporate Citizens, according to *Business Ethics*, and as one of the top 30 companies for executive women by the National Association of Female Executives.

At JetBlue Airways, a key part of the onboarding experience for new crew members consists of a heavy dose of the leadership, which shows up to welcome each new hire. It's the visibility of that leadership that gets the biggest "wow" during orientation. We participated in a new-hire orientation, and, sure enough, CEO David Neeleman, President David Barger, and Vice President and CLO Mike Barger visited the group. Much like the new employees, we were excited about meeting the bigwigs; but, after a while, we realized that they're just people like us.

PEOPLE = PROFIT: PROOF THAT IT WORKS

JetBlue Airways is a low-fare, low-cost passenger airline known for its high-quality customer service and amenities, such as seatback satellite television. JetBlue operates a fleet of European-made Airbus A320s and Brazilian-made Embraer 190s. Based at New York City's John F. Kennedy International Airport, the airline currently operates almost 400 flights a day and serves 34 destinations in 13 states, the Bahamas, the Dominican Republic, and Puerto Rico. For five years, JetBlue has claimed the top spot in the Airline Quality Rating report. It has also finished first in J. D. Power rankings for customer satisfaction.

Southwest Airlines' leaders are legendary for being available to employees. The vice president of customer relations was known for delivering paychecks every two weeks to more than 300 employees in his department, just so he could personally thank them for their hard work and service. It's common practice for Southwest leaders to walk around and interact on a first-name basis, keeping an open door and an open mind. Every year on the Wednesday before Thanksgiving, the busiest travel day of the year, company executives join the front lines to work with their employees. They understand that their primary responsibility is to encourage and support their people.

SAS leaders, too, are highly accessible and involved in the work product. Because SAS managers work alongside their employees, they understand what their groups do and can help set realistic deadlines with their teams. Founder Jim Goodnight still takes an active part in developing code and maintaining software applications. He often walks through the halls, offering to help employees with bugs they have found or code that isn't working quite right. How many software industry CEOs are that aligned with the employee experience?

> > *Would your employees describe your leadership style as accessible? Do you make it a point to know your employees as people, not just employees?*

Not What They Say but What They Do

Everybody likes to create mission and value statements. Companies post them on the walls, on their Web sites, in employee communications—wherever they have an audience. These statements may sound great; but, often, they're not real.

Scott was visiting a retail company that had placed several colorful posters on the wall by the front desk. The posters highlighted the five core principles of the entire organization—with the word trust at the top of the list. Yet, whenever people entered and exited the building, guards in blue uniforms inspected their bags and briefcases. The most important principle of the organization was being broken each time an employee entered or left the building. These types of inconsistent messages—saying one thing but doing another—erode trust and trigger an instant disconnect.

Some companies put values and principles in place for opportunistic reasons instead of for a sense of true purpose and meaning. These principles are designed for the exclusive purpose of making money, not to complete the customer and employee experience. It's a costly misalignment and a frustrating way to do business.

> > *Do leaders in your organization really "walk the talk" or just "talk the talk"?*

Companies that claim to have one set of values but live by another create stress at every level of the organization. A consultant for a leading Manhattan-based company tells a story of mis-placed priorities. A vice president lost a laptop valued at $1,100. The loss prompted a flurry of memos and meetings, even though the laptop was an outdated model containing no important doc-uments. "The organization lost 19 people in three months, but no one seemed concerned about that," he points out. "They cared much more about the $1,100 computer. It sent a clear mes-sage to all about what the company really values—things over people."

So many companies still subscribe to the "you're lucky to work here" mentality. This perspective moves through the organization at every level, ultimately disconnecting people from the business. It's a perspective that never taps into employ-ees' full potential to make money, and, in the end, it undermines the bottom line.

>> *How do you thank people for making money for your organization?*

When leaders believe their employees should be grateful for working for them, it creates an unnecessary hierarchy that erodes trust. This problem is at its worst when organizations tell employees they are their best asset, and, then, at the first sign of financial woes, drop employees from the organization as a cost-cutting measure. Unless your business is experiencing some extreme change in revenue generation, we do not ever recom-mend a reduction in head count. In those rare cases when you do need to cut jobs, we hope you've considered all other options available to you.

Employees will disconnect from an organization when they believe they'll be discarded when financial pressure hits the organization. They'll have no interest in helping the company make money. While there are no employment guarantees in today's marketplace, there nevertheless must be a perception of respect for employees.

> >> *If you've ever needed to reduce your workforce, did you provide your employees with a dignified separation process?*

Retreat or Advance

In most organizations, the problem-solving effort often happens like this: Managers have an annual meeting. They go on a retreat to discuss problems that affect everyone in the organization. Typically, no one mentions the really important issues for fear of looking bad. But flip charts abound, and fancy consultants speak on how others approach the process.

Everybody gets excited. Participants are well fed, fired up, and ready to tackle the issues they left behind at the office two days ago. They complete the event with a celebration of great food and drinks.

Once they're back at the desk, though, the cool-looking binders go on a shelf. And it's back to what they've been doing all along. Back to the same behaviors they spent two days talking about changing.

So what's missing? First, it's that retreats are called "retreats" instead of "advances." You can't fix an organization into anything, much less profitability. It is very difficult to be strategic when problem solving—you can be innovative, but strategy is reserved for building, not fixing. Advancement must come from within; organizations must learn to reinvent themselves. Instead of retreats that focus on constraints, advances help organizations talk about what they do really well and decide how they can do more of it.

>> *Does your organization hold retreats? Or does it go on advances?*

Here's a snapshot of one advance that produced extraordinary results. A marketing VP took her team members on an advance to thank them for their outstanding achievements that year and to reinforce the behaviors that contributed to their success. We assisted them in creating an agenda and a facilitation strategy: employee–customer connection activities that focused on individual and team accomplishments and ways for them to capture their positive actions on an ongoing basis. The only things not allowed on the agenda were the usual retreat topics—business metrics, competitive activities, and "where we missed the target" kinds of discussions. The group was whisked away to an open field, where a hot-air balloon was ready to ascend. The balloon ride symbolized the team members' "sky's the limit" approach—and their ability to go above and beyond expectations. They toted a miniature version of the balloon back to the office. Today, the basket of the balloon on display is used as a collection point for new ideas, acknowledgments, and recognition and reinforces the memory of the team's productive advance.

We are not suggesting that you ignore your problems. Rather, we are suggesting that you find the balance of "fixing" and "building." Fixing only gets you back to where you should have been; but it doesn't get you to where you need to be—that must be built. And to build we must look ahead and leverage our strengths as well as deal with our challenges.

A manufacturing company held an advance with the customer service and distribution teams to acknowledge each function's independent contributions to the customer experience. The teams discussed how they could combine their efforts to create a synergistic, altruistic approach of serving instead of simply providing service. This was the first time the teams had an opportunity to come together to talk about how their collective efforts created the total customer experience and how they could improve processes and response time.

> >> How can your next management advance focus on what your organization does really well and how you can do more of it? How can you stop fixing and start building?

Not Looking Stupid

Many organizations see information as power, and they dole it out to their people on a need-to-know basis. Yet, people who don't fully understand what's expected of them may easily disengage because they don't know the organization's Destination or understand their part in it. Often, they're afraid to ask questions because it's more important to look credible than to admit that they don't know.

"Tell me what I want to hear instead of what I really need to know" is what you get when the environment is one of fear, intimidation, and personal agendas. Rather than questioning the status quo—what we call the "stagnant quo"—people try to avoid looking stupid.

W. L. Gore is masterful at questioning the stagnant quo. At this problem-solving company, grounded in technical competence, people are encouraged to ask questions and take risks. Everyone at Gore, every day, strives to create new solutions or applications that expand the boundaries of what technology can do. One of the company's key commitments is that its products will do what it says they will do. From cables that deploy airbags to winter coats that keep you dry, Gore makes the best things possible. And, to do that, it needs the best people possible.

At Gore, there is no fear of looking stupid. The company believes that if you build devoted, enthusiastic teams, they will create great business results. These results feed back into the organization, producing a higher level of energy and a passion to continue to do more. Gore calls its communication structure a "lattice," which means that everyone—regardless of his or her role in the organization—is encouraged to speak directly with anyone else in the organization. This open-door policy ignites high trust because leaders are available to listen to associates informally.

> >> *Do people in your organization feel that they can speak up? Can they ask the right questions without fear of looking stupid?*

Your Destination

If any company is to find success, it needs to know where it's going. This may be defined through a mission statement, a strategic plan, and so on. Whatever the vehicle, we refer to the end goal as a Destination, with a capital D. Unlike a goal or a strategy, a Destination has two key imperatives:

- You need to know exactly where you're going.

- You need to find the best route to get there.

When everyone in the company understands the Destination, all will contribute to the journey.

As your business grows and the market changes, your Destinations may be many. Increased profitability. A bigger market share. Cultural change. Recognition for being an excellent employer or for having a great workplace.

Let's say one of your Destinations is to be the top provider of your service or to hold the best-selling SKU for your product category. While these are admirable Destinations, they're Destinations your competitors want, too. It's not uncommon for organizations to have the same Destinations. So what will help you get there before your competition does? And, once you are there, what will sustain you? We believe it's your people.

Believing Is Seeing

Once you have defined your Destination, you need to help others visualize it. A picture is worth way more than a thousand words. So go ahead and paint one for your people, so vividly clear that they believe it because you can see it. And you help them see it.

Who doesn't remember the jingle "two all-beef patties, special sauce, lettuce, cheese, pickles, onion on a sesame-seed bun"? McDonald's got an entire nation to see that and say it. FedEx succeeded in painting the picture of overnight delivery, even though it would cost much, much more than sending a letter. The early critics thought no one would use FedEx. Today, who doesn't? Southwest Airlines got its people to believe that they, not just the plane ride, are the value proposition their customers pay for. Who hasn't told one of those crazy Southwest flight stories? Southwest's people see the Destination every day, and they deliver on it.

Sunny Vanderbeck, CEO of technology leader Data Return, has painted a compelling picture for his staff of 250. Data Return's Destination, Vanderbeck explains, is to improve the lives of people who use and deploy IT—not only IT directors and chief information officers but the people who use the technology every day. "We're constantly looking for ways to make their lives easier and take their pain away," Vanderbeck says, "so their pager doesn't go off at three in the morning when they're on vacation with their families, bearing the bad news that their mission-critical application is down." Can you imagine what happens when an entire organization believes that it exists solely to improve the lives of people who use IT?

PEOPLE = PROFIT: PROOF THAT IT WORKS

Data Return is a privately owned information technology company headquartered in Dallas, Texas. Founded in 1996, the company has enjoyed remarkable success in establishing itself as the leading provider of managed hosting services for companies using a variety of platforms. Under the leadership of CEO Sunny Vanderbeck, Data Return has grown from a technology start-up to a $65 million company with more than 250 employees. Vanderbeck has been recognized as a visionary in the managed hosting industry and has twice been named by Ernst & Young as one of the top 25 technology leaders in Dallas.

>> *What pictures of your Destinations are you painting for your people? Are the pictures so clear that they know you believe it, and do they believe it, too?*

The Financial Equation

How many times does a manager say, "Why trouble our front-line workers with business details? They don't need to know about our internal operations and financial happenings." But how can people intentionally behave in a way that's good for the business if they don't understand how their company makes money—and, more specifically, how their jobs fit into the equation? How can they help if they don't know what is going on?

> > *Do people know what's really important to your business? Are they pooling their collective energy in pursuit of those things?*

Southwest Airlines makes it a practice to keep employees informed about the company's financial position. For example, during an economic slowdown, Southwest leaders realized they needed to reduce the budget by several million dollars. Along with enrolling department heads to trim budgets, the company took a more inclusive approach. It sent a personal letter to every employee. The message was, We're all in this together. We need each of you to find a way to save $5 a day.

Instead of being a management edict, which usually creates an atmosphere of uncertainty and disdain, saving money became an involving and fun employee experience. People wanted to participate. Individuals and teams competed enthusiastically to find ways to save more.

Southwest surpassed the targeted goal in record time. The initiative succeeded because people were well connected to Southwest and were engaged in its success. Each Southwest employee was approached as a partner in the business, and they all responded like business partners! They knew that if they succeeded in saving, the company would succeed, too.

Southwest also makes it a point to quantify the value of every employee activity. Financial information is readily available. Employees know how many customers are needed on each plane to break even and how many to be profitable. They know the cost of fuel and supplies and the cost of a flight delay. In sum, they know the cost of doing business and the profit earned by performing their jobs on time and on budget. In fact, Southwest employees own 15 percent of the company through a profit-sharing plan that has paid continuous dividends.

The law firm Alston & Bird (A&B) shares financial information in its periodic town meetings with employees. "You don't have to be a partner to know what's going on financially with all our practices," says Cathy Benton, chief people officer. Alston & Bird believes that when employees understand the financial picture of their organization, they're better equipped to do their jobs more effectively.

PEOPLE = PROFIT: PROOF THAT IT WORKS

Alston & Bird is a major U.S. law firm with an extensive national and international practice. Founded in 1893, the firm has more than 675 attorneys located in offices in Georgia, New York, North Carolina, and Washington, D.C., offering services in virtually every practice area from antitrust to wealth planning. The firm was ranked number two in 2004 and number nine in 2005 on *Fortune*'s 100 Best Companies to Work For list and is the first and only law firm ever named to the top five.

East Alabama Medical Center (EAMC), one of the only public hospitals to be selected for *Fortune*'s 100 Best Companies to Work For list, connects its people to the financial equation through a gain-sharing program. When EAMC reaches its financial goals, employees receive an annual bonus check, up to 5 percent of their salaries. By understanding the financial side of the business, employees are motivated to have an intentional impact on the bottom line.

Sallie Mae talks with its employees about financial results every three months—at the same time it announces results to shareholders. "We want our employees to understand what the company is doing, and we want to thank them for their efforts," explains Joni Reich, senior vice president of administration. "We want to reinforce that they really are the heartbeat of our organization."

SC Johnson (SCJ) has had a profit-sharing program since 1917. Profit sharing includes everyone, from the production line to the executive offices. "It was a decision that illustrated the SC Johnson way, which is that we are truly all in this together," says Kelly Semrau, vice president of global public affairs and communication. It's no wonder that SCJ employees have unusually long tenures. In short, people don't want to leave!

PEOPLE = PROFIT: PROOF THAT IT WORKS

SC Johnson, one of the world's leading manufacturers of household cleaning products and products for home storage, air care, personal care, and insect control, markets its products in more than 100 countries. Established in 1886, the company is family owned and managed, with operations in over 70 countries. For decades, the company's heritage of corporate leadership in environmental and social responsibility has been recognized by governments and nongovernmental organizations around the world. SC Johnson employs 12,000 people worldwide and has annual estimated sales of more than $6.5 billion.

>> *Do people understand how your organization makes money? Do they share financially in its success?*

Savings through Investing in People

Organizations that have succeeded in connecting the people to the business have reported bottom-line savings. SAS's employee amenities not only create happier employees but save the company about $75 million each year. SAS founder Goodnight believes that "you can either pay headhunters or give the money to employees."

Jeff Chambers, vice president of human resources at SAS, reports that the company's on-site health care center brings direct and indirect savings. "Directly, the center yields savings of $1 million over the cost of a for-profit medical center. Indirectly, it saves us money because having access to free care means employees are sick less often and, therefore, more productive." The average SAS employee takes two and a half sick days a year, Chambers says. The center also produces savings in time lost traveling to and from the doctor's office. The average doctor visit at the SAS site takes 20 minutes, compared to an average of 90 minutes off-site—yielding annual savings of at least eight figures.

In the long term, SAS expects to save money on health expenses as its employee population continues to age. (The average age now is 43.) "We believe this population, as it ages, will be healthier," Chambers predicts. "We think we'll have lower incidences of catastrophic health claims for chronic conditions because we give our employees what they need, on-site, to manage their health."

SAS continues to add new benefits as employee needs arise. It has an ad hoc group that meets to discuss proposed new benefits and programs. The group evaluates proposals based on three points: Will the benefit fit with SAS culture? Will it serve a significant number of employees? and Will it be cost-effective? Bene-fits that would cause the company to spend more than it saves, as was true for a suggested on-site pharmacy and a doggie daycare center, are nixed. (SAS is, however, negotiating discount programs at external doggie daycare centers for employees.)

Human Beings versus Human Doings

People are looking for ways to find more peace in their lives and time for more "being," not just more "doing." The harsh reality today is that companies often make employees choose between family and work—which is always a losing proposition.

Winning organizations are helping their people be "human beings," rather than feel like "human doings." They're treating their people as whole persons, always in a developing process—understanding that a person's needs are the same inside the workplace as they are outside the workplace.

It's no coincidence that we're seeing a movement toward training that speaks to the whole person. Many companies are offering such courses as "How to Talk to Your Teenagers," "How to Be a Great Single Parent," and "Finding the Artist Within." Is this tied to the business? You bet it is! Investing in the total person is an excellent way to expand that person's success on the job, too. Savvy organizations know that better human beings make better employees. The more developed the person, the more developed the employee will be and the more able to deliver even higher performance for your organization.

> >> What programs are in place at your organization to help people have a quality life at work and a quality life at home?

SAS offers a work-life center with programs that address the issues its people are most concerned about, from raising children and taking care of aging parents to planning financially for the future. "We want our employees to get the help they need with the issues they face. That way, they're not burdened by them and can be more effective when they're on the job," says Jeff Chambers, vice president of human resources.

Perkins Coie, an innovative law firm in business since 1912, is well known for its people practices. Employees have the opportunity to determine how much time they want to work because the firm believes in a balance between home life and work life, according to Darrin Emmerick, chief personnel officer. Associates guarantee the number of hours they'll work in a year, and if they work over the designated amount, they're rewarded with a bonus. This signals an extraordinary shift in law firms from a business model of "billable hours" to giving lawyers a choice.

PEOPLE = PROFIT: PROOF THAT IT WORKS

Perkins Coie, the largest law practice in the Pacific Northwest, has more than 600 attorneys in 14 offices across the United States and in Asia. The firm represents clients ranging in size from Fortune 100 companies to start-ups and has historically represented market leaders in traditional and cutting-edge technology industries. Through its Community Service Fellowship, the firm donates the full-time services of attorneys on behalf of community organizations in the arts, human services, education, health care, and indigent legal services. Perkins Coie was named one of *Fortune*'s Best Companies to Work For in 2005.

*"Our approach is to help people be successful
in all walks of life, not just on the job. We
know they won't be effective at work if
they're having problems at home."*

—Terry Andrus, CEO, East Alabama Medical Center

East Alabama Medical Center offers a self-help group that assists employees in solving their life problems. CEO Terry Andrus tells the story of an LPN and single mother who called to say that her husband was threatening her. Within an hour, the director of the self-help group, Jean Causey, followed up with the employee. Causey made arrangements to help her find new housing and make sure the woman was protected if threatened again. "We could have ignored her and said, essentially, 'It's not our problem. It's your problem,'" says Andrus. "But that's not how we do things here."

PEOPLE = PROFIT: PROOF THAT IT WORKS

East Alabama Medical Center, founded in 1952, is a 334-bed acute care regional comprehensive medical facility. It is owned and operated by the East Alabama Health Care Authority. EAMC has about 2,500 staff members, including nearly 150 staff physicians with specialties in virtually every medical field. Facilities also include two outpatient diagnostic centers, a community education center, home health services, a hospice facility, an adult daycare center, a cancer center, a sleep disorders lab, a pediatric unit, and a wellness and fitness facility. EAMC has twice made *Fortune*'s 100 Best Companies to Work For list, the first public-sector agency ever to make the list.

Dallas-based TD Industries, plumbing and air-conditioning contractors, has also mastered the art of treating people as human beings first. With the top company value a "concern for and belief in individual human beings," TD Industries views customers as the engine that drives its ability to provide "outstanding careers for all employee owners and security for their families"—which is the company's mission. In an industry that isn't known for being people-focused, TD Industries has taken on the mandate to grow people—and has made tremendous profits doing it.

> >> How do you encourage your employees to be success-
> ful in all walks of life?

The Purpose-Driven Job

In today's information age, we're surrounded by stimulation, yet most of us are still starved for meaning. People say over and over that what matters most to them in the workplace isn't money. It's meaning. Pay and benefits aren't enough to motivate the right people. They want to feel good about themselves and the work they're doing. Money becomes a priority only when meaning is missing.

University of Massachusetts research professor Robert Weiss asked people whether they would work if they inherited enough money to live out their lives, and 8 out of 10 said yes.[3] Then there are those who have generated enough wealth through their businesses to retire early but still choose to work. Does Bill Gates show up each day for a paycheck?

Some industries have a built-in advantage in the meaning department. Ask a firefighter or an emergency medical technician about the meaning in their jobs, and you're likely to get a ready answer: "I save lives." At U.S. Customs and Border Protection (CBP), meaning couldn't be clearer for the agency's 30,000 agents. "Our people realize they're our nation's defense against global terrorism," says CBP Commissioner Robert Bonner. "No other government agency has a more important mission."

PEOPLE = PROFIT: PROOF THAT IT WORKS

U.S. Customs and Border Protection is the unified border agency within the Department of Homeland Security. The agency is charged with managing, controlling, and protecting U.S. borders at and between official ports of entry and with keeping terrorists and terrorist weapons out of the country while enforcing hundreds of U.S. laws. With its One Face at the Border initiative, launched after 9/11, CBP successfully integrated four different organizations from three different government departments, with no interruption in operations. The 42,000-employee agency represents one-fourth of employees in the Department of Homeland Security.

People count on their leaders to create the kind of workplace where they feel valued, appreciated, and part of something bigger than their jobs. Whatever your product or service, helping people find meaning in what they're doing is essential to giving them a sense of lasting connection to the company. That may be as simple as demonstrating how the products they make, the services they support, or the work they do is actually used in the world. Without this understanding, what they do each day may always feel like just a job.

At Corning, employees are motivated by their ability to change the world through invention and innovation. "Innovation has been the backbone of the company since its inception," says Gail Baity, vice president of human resources. "We take pride that, in every decade, we have done something for humankind." It's a tradition that stretches back to 1879, when inventor Thomas Edison came to Corning looking for glass for his incandescent lamp. The result? Cutting-edge technology for the world's first lightbulb.

PEOPLE = PROFIT: PROOF THAT IT WORKS

Corning Incorporated, founded in 1851, develops life-changing innovations, beginning with the glass for Thomas Edison's lightbulb in 1879. Today, the company is a leading manufacturer of optical fiber and cable systems for the telecommunications industry and high-performance flat glass for television and information display applications. Corning also develops advanced materials for the scientific, semiconductor, and environmental industries. With research centers around the world and more than 70 manufacturing locations, the Corning team has about 25,000 employees.

At Alston & Bird, it's "not just about billable hours," says Cathy Benton, chief human resources officer. With 700 attorneys and 1,500 total employees, A&B has the reputation of being a place where "the good people work." Just ask the many lawyers and other staff members who have migrated to A&B from other firms because they were attracted to A&B's people principles. "You can be a great place to work and a profitable organization," Benton says, "but what really makes the difference is if you have happy employees who will really take care of your business."

Benton tells the story of Mr. Miller, one of Alston & Bird's founders and perhaps its happiest-ever employee. He came to work every day until he was 90 years old; in the last few years, he came in just to have lunch and connect with the firm's people. "It would take him forever to walk through the building to get to the dining room," she remembers. "Then, we'd see him holding court with all these young attorneys, just talking about the practice of law. They were in awe of him." Today, managing partner Ben Johnson carries on the tradition of a purpose-driven, people-focused practice—one that hasn't had a layoff since its founding in 1882.

"Without our people, we have nothing to offer.
They are the driving force behind our organization."
—Ben Johnson, Managing Partner, Alston & Bird

>> *How do people at your organization know that their*
work is meaningful?

One Interaction at a Time

The bottom line is this: It's no longer an option to disregard the power of the people. They determine whether the business lives or dies. As CEOs come and go, the only constant is the people who serve your customers every day.

Creating a connected culture may seem overwhelming, but it's really very simple. Influence is created one interaction at a time. That's how employees measure the health of their workplace experience—one interaction at a time. It could be with their CEO, supervisor, colleague, customer, or vendor. Every leader has an enormous opportunity to shape and define the employee experience every time there's an interaction in the organization.

>> *How is your organization shaping the employee*
experience, one interaction at a time?

A hundred interactions a day are a hundred opportunities to connect people with the business. At the end of the day, if you've made a hundred connections—with colleagues, bosses, and customers—and each interaction is a good one, it begins to add up exponentially to shape your people experience in such a way that profits begin to flow.

[2] PATHWAYS TO PROFITABILITY

Finding a New Way

In today's dynamic and global economy, companies cannot compete in the same old ways. They need to find innovative ways of leveraging opportunity by connecting their people to their businesses like never before. It's not only about being profitable but also about doing the right thing, because we find that doing the right thing is an excellent source of pride and connection to business growth and, ultimately, profit.

In the months after 9/11, many of us began to ponder our hectic lives, our 12-hour workdays, and those rare appearances at home. More important, we were reminded of what really matters to us.

It wasn't a shift to thinking of work as unimportant, but, rather, a realization that other things are important, too. A chilling reminder of how precious life really is, 9/11 seemed to awaken the humanity of a country and, perhaps, a world. Many turned to the workplace to get connected, to find meaning in their lives, and to ensure that what was important to them personally was also recognized as important in their work. This may have meant spending less time traveling, leaving the office at a regular time every day, or maybe even taking the vacation that's offered each year but that many people simply let slip by.

As employees seek to connect more to both their jobs and their lives, employers are realizing that connecting people to the business is a must-do. Technology has made it much easier for competitors to take your most prized assets away from you: your people and your customers. So providing a workplace that enables your people to feel better about the world is not only a lofty goal but a workplace essential. At the end of the day, everyone wants to count.

Opportunities to connect your people to something important are plentiful and happen in many ways. Connection can be through the product or service you provide, the workplace experience you offer, the perceived good you do in the world, or the social responsibility your company demonstrates in the community. There are endless ways to connect people to your business and keep them connected to your customers as well as your profits. When true connection happens, it's a win for everyone.

In our work with organizations that focus on connecting people to their business performance, we've uncovered seven Pathways to Profitability. We'll explore these Pathways here, with a few suggestions on how successful organizations are working through them. In later chapters, we'll look in depth at how these companies are putting the Pathways to work.

Pathway #1: Get the Right Destination

You can't get to where you're going if you don't know where it is. The first requirement in connecting people to your business, then, is to have a clear Destination for your organization. Nothing is more frustrating than to have a bunch of great individuals being great individuals when you need them to be a team and to work toward a collective win for your organization.

Is this something you've heard before? We thought so. What exactly is it that keeps your organization's leadership from setting the direction with such clarity that everyone in the organization knows it, feels it, shapes his or her agenda around it, and ultimately reaches it?

A company that competes well in today's aggressive and chaotic environment knows not only its Destination but also the most direct route to it and steers everyone in the same direction in order to get there. While this may be like herding cats, it's a fundamental in the organizational competencies of making money. Lack of focus on a Destination creates extreme stress in an organization and causes it to perform poorly in the short and long terms. The goal is to establish a Destination that's vividly clear to employees and other stakeholders and to ensure that goals look and feel—and are—attainable. If a goal is too lofty, employees will find it unrealistic, confirming their worst fears about management: Leadership "doesn't get it" and is completely out of touch.

Does an organization need to have just one Destination? No. In fact, your organization will have multiple Destinations. Individuals will be working toward their Destinations, and teams will be working toward their Destinations. Organizational Destinations, however, must shape individual and team Destinations or should at least be the converging point for activity. Because the most critical Destinations are those that fulfill the organization's goals, it's important that individuals and teams funnel their behaviors, actions, and focus toward the larger Destination. Should there be any deviation, you must review the plan and assess the potential effects on the overall organizational goal. If an organization's goal is to create a great workplace that attracts and retains top talent, then each team in the organization can begin to fully embrace this Destination, acting in ways that create a great workplace every day. Leaders also need to think about the goal at the individual level, understand what it will take for every person to experience the organization as "great," and then work toward that every day.

Part of the reason organizations fail to deliver is that they have competing priorities, and not everyone really understands what to do next. Remember, you not only need to have the "most right" Destination possible; you need to ensure that everyone buys into it, a point we'll discuss in chapter 5.

Whatever your organization's Destinations, they need to be seen and understood at all levels, included in every agenda, and woven into every business discussion and decision. Although this is a challenging request, imagine the greater challenge of trying to clean up the mess resulting from a misaligned organization!

A Destination that's really working for an organization brings something magical. When Starbucks said that one of its Destinations was to be a "third place" where all of us could go, along with our homes and our offices, Starbucks employees began creating that experience for their customers. (If you ask Starbucks what they sell, you won't hear the word *coffee*. Starbucks sells an experience.) In communities everywhere, Starbucks readily transformed into a third place—the place we go to grab a morning coffee, have an afternoon cup of tea, or check e-mail with the stores' T-Mobile wireless Internet service.

You may have also noticed another very intentional focus for Starbucks. You typically see the same servers—or baristas, as they're called in the coffee world—serving you each time you stop by. Why? Starbucks has managed to connect them to the business in a way that makes them want to stay. In fact, you may have a favorite Starbucks where the baristas know your name and have your latte ready before you can order it. Sounds like home, right? Exactly. It's their way of building a relationship with you so that you're more likely to see them as your third place. Familiarity brews sales: When you view Starbucks as that third place, you're nine times more likely to purchase more of their products.

"Chunking," a Great Way to Go

Organizations often find themselves paralyzed by the sheer magnitude of determining a Destination. While we strongly advocate attainable and meaningful Destinations, at times you need to dream big and go after something you know isn't readily attainable today but will be in the future. We encourage a plan that "chunks" Destinations, that is, breaks down the parts of a larger, longer-term Destination into smaller, more manageable parts so that your workforce is mobilized rather than put in a frenzy. You might set an ultimate Destination of having stores in all 50 states within 10 years. Your chunked Destinations might be to target 5 states each year—a much less intimidating plan.

Don't try the impossible, at least all at once. If your Destination is to be first in market share, but you're dead last in your category today, a more realistic Destination might be to stay in business. This type of Destination is hard to share with the organization. Yet, if it's realistic, you may want to consider the potential of something this basic. People love reality, even though they're not used to getting it from management. Why? Because no one likes to admit failure, and everyone loves to bask in success. So we tend to sugarcoat the hard stuff. But employees usually figure out what's really going on, and this sometimes makes management look like it's hiding something. Sharing a goal such as staying in business is always tricky, yet we find being straightforward is a refreshing and successful approach for leaders.

Imagine the galvanizing force it will have on your people! Everyone loves to work for a cause. What better cause than your own organization? In the uncertainty that followed 9/11, Southwest Airlines decided to uphold its 33-year history of no layoffs, unlike many companies that immediately laid off thousands. Southwest's people have always rallied during crises, and 9/11 proved the ultimate test of commitment. Executives gave up their pay from September through December, and employees offered payroll deductions exceeding $2 million. Loyal Southwest customers told Southwest to keep the money for canceled flights instead of refunding it. If Southwest had been only about "flights," do you think customers would have done this?

Another Destination that might need to be chunked is a major cultural shift, perhaps building a great workplace. Certainly this is a good Destination to consider, assuming it leverages your Optimum People-Profit Opportunities, discussed in chapter 4, or helps create more income for your organization. Since this Destination will require significant changes in all levels, departments, processes, and procedures, you may want to start with a chunk that simply defines your current culture or perhaps what you mean when you say "great workplace." Once your definition is in place and understood by all, you may continue toward achieving the Destination of a great workplace.

Many years ago, a client's leadership team approached us. Leaders were convinced that their company needed to be a great workplace. We met with the team several times, only to find that the organizational culture was in a turmoil caused by fear and politicking; the company was far from being a great workplace. We made our case that the goal was simply too aggressive for the moment and recommended that leaders focus on something more realistic. They were coached to reduce their 236 percent turnover and focus on the everyday experience of their people. "It would be a start," we said, "to have your people greet each other in the hallways."

We recommended that their first organizational Destination be to implement the value of respect in all that they did. From hiring to onboarding, to daily interactions and coaching, it all centered on respect. Nearly four years later, this company is a good place to work and has recently begun to move toward being a great place.

> > *If you have several Destinations, which is the most important? Which is immediate? Which is long-term?*

Down the Wrong Road

Before you set your Destination, you need to think through whether it is the right one for your company. You may read some of the stories in this book and think, "I'll try that with my company." Be warned that most Destinations are not cookie-cutter goals. They must be carefully molded to fit your company, or they may have negative results.

Many companies have tried to emulate SAS Institute, setting the Destination of developing highly productive people by adding employee amenities. Both competitors and noncompetitors have hastily added perks like pools and massages, believing these will make their employees as happy and productive as those at SAS. Perks are one way of connecting people to the business; but, unless that fundamental emotional and psychological connection is there, no amount of perks and benefits can give you a significant return. If you have a low-trust culture and you try to implement an on-site massage program, you'll be wasting time and money. If trust is low, people may not take advantage of the benefit, assuming you're testing them to see who chooses to keep working and who takes a break to get a massage. Perks won't engage employees who are otherwise disengaged, or as Data Return CEO Sunny Vanderbeck says, "If you're putting frosting on a cake that tastes bad, it doesn't work."

Sometimes, when you embark on a journey, things happen along the way. Customer needs change, new opportunities arise, new information comes to light. You need to continually evaluate progress and make corrections as needed.

In the early 1990s, W. L. Gore & Associates had an informal Destination: Make money now. It was a good Destination in many ways, because the company needed the cash flow. Yet, in making money now, it was less able to focus on R&D and long-term planning. Several years later, Gore's leaders realized they had not been feeding the product pipeline adequately, making the company more vulnerable to competition. Their original Destination had created some challenges. In typical Gore fashion, the company used its ability to innovate to reset the Destination in plenty of time, staying well ahead of the competition. Because the goal of making money in the short term challenged the company's ability to outpace its competitors, Gore's leaders shifted the Destination to one that enabled more profitability through a long-term focus on superior products.

Gore's experience teaches us a valuable lesson: Any Destination may bring new challenges, which must be assessed and incorporated into the overall plan for success. Gore's distinctive and innovative culture enabled it to quickly refocus efforts on R&D, communicate this broadened focus to the entire organization—literally overnight through its lattice communication structure—and continue to out-innovate its competitors in every market.

>> *How do you communicate your Destination
  to your people?*

The Core Issue

Eventually, chunk Destinations will help achieve some larger Destination, such as meeting the need for enhanced profit margins, increasing branding awareness, or helping employees be more effective. If your Destination won't solve a major problem for your organization or your primary customers, you probably have the wrong Destination, or at least one that's not as "right" as it could be.

One method used to determine a Destination is to understand the core issue. Most people are good at problem-solving. In fact, they may be too good at the solving part compared to the problem part. Managers are eager to solve problems and fix things. It's one of the tasks they've been hired to do. Yet, being gifted at solving problems is different from being gifted at identifying problems—that is, finding the real core issue. Solving the wrong issue is common in organizations because the solving may be equated with success regardless of whether it resolves the core issue. Finding the core issue is essential in today's business environment, as there simply isn't enough time to solve the wrong problems. You know you've solved the wrong problem when the symptoms that alerted you to the issue persist or return.

A major fast-food restaurant chain had a 243 percent annual turnover in employees working the cash registers. This was quite high compared to the industry average of 154 percent. After the company experimented with several solutions, we were asked to assess the problem and try to understand why these employees in particular were so disconnected from the organization that they simply quit. We met with representatives from all positions in the restaurants, with special emphasis on cashiers, the highest turnover position. Although it seems obvious to us now, the major difference between the cashiers and everyone else turned out to be that these employees had an enormous amount of interaction with customers. And, for better or worse, they bore the brunt of any customer complaints, about the food, the bathrooms, and even parking-space limitations!

We eventually found that the often young cashiers were quitting because they didn't have the life skills to handle the rejection that came with complaints—a common occurrence for customer service employees. The company decided to initiate training on developing a positive self-image and defusing angry customers. It led to a dramatic drop in turnover as well as a new onboarding program designed to set up cashiers to succeed. The program focused on getting more customers to return to the restaurant and helping cashiers learn to recover quickly when something went wrong. Getting at the core issue of helping employees overcome rejection ensured that training dollars were spent on the issue most critical to employee retention. This armed the leadership team with the information it needed to create Destinations that were focused on the core issues.

A customer called a manufacturer of electronic products and asked, "Do you have calendars over there?" The inside salesperson taking the call, known for her excellence in customer service, quickly replied, "I'm not sure. I'll check." She then ran all over the plant hoping to find an extra copy of the company calendar to send to her customer. She stopped by HR. She called the public relations department, but there was no company calendar to be found. Disappointed, she picked up the phone again and informed the customer, "No, we don't have calendars here."

The customer was enraged. Not about the calendar, but because his shipment was late and he had called to complain, starting with, "Do you have calendars . . . ?" This was a clear signal from the customer, but the inside salesperson missed it and spent time solving the wrong problem. Her customer was even more upset by the long hold and what he perceived as a brash response from this seasoned salesperson. All the while, the employee thought she was doing the right thing. However, she had totally missed the signal!

>> *How good are your people at identifying core issues?*

We believe that the best, and quickest, way to get to the core issues is to adopt a "needs-first, solutions-second" approach, discussed in chapter 4. The evolution of a business produces many issues that must be resolved. As external customers demand more and different things from organizations, organizations must be in the business of understanding needs and then applying solutions to those needs. Had the inside salesperson listened to everything the customer was saying, including the tone and nonverbal signals, she would have heard the actual need. Sometimes, though, just as you get everyone to understand the needs, someone leaves the team or organization, new people enter, and you have to start the process over again. It's critical, then, that you teach, role-model, and expect employees to work toward uncovering needs and core issues in every interaction, both internal and external—and then apply a solution.

>> *Do you constantly look for the needs first and then look for and apply solutions?*

Pathway #2: Connect People to the Business

Generally, there are three types of employees: the dedicated go-getters who contribute no matter what, the not-so-dedicated no-getters who do the minimum work necessary to get by, and those in between who could be strong contributors if only they received attention and understood the importance of their work. Their fates hinge on how you choose to engage them and connect them to the business.

How many of your employees come in each day willing to tear down walls for your organization? They're the ones who make things happen, have unwavering commitment, and never give less than 100 percent. Have you identified these people for your organization? Are they your top talent? Do you let them know they're your top talent? These people are the key to profitability. Keeping them connected is absolutely essential to your organization's ability to outpace your competitors.

If you know who these employees are, please send us their names and contact information and a brief description of why they're so good. We'll send each of them a personal note thanking them for their contributions to your organization and inviting them to share their stories as examples for others. You can contact us at www.DestinationProfit.com.

Along with your top talent, you may have other employees who do not want to give anything more to your organization than is absolutely necessary, who only want to come in and do their jobs. They're in every organization and can be a costly investment of resources. We are often asked how many employees of this type are acceptable in an organization. To us, that depends on how many employees of this type your competitors have working for them. If they have about 10 percent of their workforce just showing up, and you have 5 percent, what a great advantage that is for you! However, if they have only 5 percent, and you have 15 percent, you have a significant disadvantage.

One way of engaging these employees is to work diligently to connect them to the organization. You also might consider putting them into new environments—a new job or a different department. Regrettably, we sometimes find that a separation is long overdue for employees who have already quit mentally and emotionally, yet remain at the job. Although this sounds harsh, the reality is that if individuals can't contribute, no one wins. Help them help the organization, or help them find a place where they can do their best work. Then everyone wins.

There are great people inside your company right now who, through no fault of theirs, are totally disconnected from the company. Because of one interaction, or perhaps several, they may believe that they or their jobs are not important to the company. Perhaps they feel they simply don't fit in. Every organization has tremendous opportunities to connect with employees, starting with its perception of them and their ability to contribute.

> *"Companies fail because they disconnect the business and people sides of the business. That's wrong. They've got to be the same thing."*
>
> —Captain Mike Barger, Vice President and
> Chief Learning Officer, JetBlue Airways

Throughout the employee life cycle, many activities can cement connections to the organization—from welcoming employees when they onboard and helping them understand the direction of the company, to celebrating and showing appreciation, to providing community service opportunities, to knowing who they are so that they can connect, through mind and heart, with what the organization really is.

The Nurturing of Key Relationships

Connecting people to the organization is an ongoing process. Each step speaks to the six business relationships we believe every company must nurture in order to function at its maximum capacity. The three primary relationships are company, supervisor, and colleagues; the three secondary relationships are job, career, and customers. Leaders need to tune in to the health of the relationship between each person and the organization. If any of these relationships is unhealthy, the organization will pay in lost revenue and waning performance.

The Company

In connecting to the company, employees need to feel they're part of the heart of what their organization is all about. They need to like being at work, care about the company, know where it's going, and want to contribute to its success.

At Sallie Mae, employees are inspired by the end product of their work. "Our mission is one people naturally want to be a part of," says Joni Reich, Sallie Mae's senior vice president of administration. "The goal of making higher education possible for millions of Americans is something people feel proud of being part of from the first day on the job. It's one of the great advantages we have as an employer—a meaningful mission."

At Data Return, employees feel an emotional connection to their work through a shared purpose. "We exist to improve the lives of people who use and deploy IT," says CEO Sunny Vanderbeck. Employees also follow their five Guiding Principles, which they collectively created in a series of intensive discussions:

1. **See things differently.** Feed your mind. Push beyond the known, the comfortable, the expected. Accept no limits. Know that everything is possible.

2. **Stand together.** Unite to achieve. Form long-term partnerships with customers and co-workers alike. Always protect these bonds. Always do the right thing.

3. **Go beyond.** Outthink, outshine, outdistance. Surpass expectations, including your own. Recognize that your performance creates your company's success. Play to win.

4. **Lead the way.** Grab the reins. Create a path where no path existed and advance with certainty. Deliver results that set you and the company apart.

5. **Adapt and evolve.** Be swift, be agile. Understand that staying in one place means falling behind. Seize change and become the future.

The Supervisor

One of the most critical links connecting people to the organization is a healthy relationship between supervisors and those they supervise. By supervisor, we mean anyone at any level who supervises another person—from a line manager to the CEO. Often, the extent of the employee's relationship with the organization is based on interactions with the supervisor, because, in many ways, for many people, the supervisor is the organization. He or she shapes each person's day-to-day experience.

People need to trust their supervisor and feel that he or she is credible and competent. Supervisors must be trustworthy, have the capabilities and confidence to manage well, set clear expectations for those they supervise, and provide meaningful feedback. For the supervisory relationship to succeed, both parties need to have the desire to do well for each other.

The supervisory relationship has a dual focus, built on tasks and the personal connection. When both focuses are good, we see results. When relationships begin to deteriorate, supervisor and employee may interact only for the purpose of completing tasks. This is a problem, because the only part of the person being acknowledged is the "doing" part, not the "being" part. It's not the right way to motivate and secure buy-in. According to research by ModernThink, in a situation where a supervisor and subordinate have a "task relationship" only, the employee will be 30 to 40 percent less effective. Relationships really matter.

We're not saying people have to love their supervisors. But both sides need to respect the task and the other person. When respect breaks down, it's difficult to get back. People will likely disconnect, not only from the supervisor, but from the entire organization. Or, they'll circumvent so their needs can be met elsewhere. That's OK, as long as they let their supervisors know what they're doing and why.

When trust is low, acknowledge it. Then, try to secure a mutual commitment to build it. The ironic thing about trust is that you can't get it until you give it. When a relationship goes bad, people tend to cross their arms and think, "I'm going to wait until I can trust this person again." Trust is never really earned; it's extended. Could there be ways for someone in the relationship to extend trust again with the hope that it will be returned? Perhaps, but if the trust is broken again, the cycle of mistrust will continue. The relationship will be poor, and so will the results.

If supervisory relationships can't be improved, look for other ways of meeting the employee's leadership needs. Look for a different supervisor. Consider ways of strengthening the other five relationships. It may be that some supervisors have poor relationships with most of the people they supervise. These are the ones who may need to be coached, redirected, or exited from the organization.

Colleagues

Colleagues are the third primary relationship. People need to feel they're integral to their group's success. Sometimes, the difference between wanting to call in sick and coming in to work is the desire to not let the team down. When relationships among colleagues are strong, we see people giving their best work. Provide the time and space for people to get to know one another. Consider team-building events or opportunities for one-on-one information-sharing.

East Alabama Medical Center has an unusual way of helping colleagues reach out to one another through its Cornerstone Society. It's an employee-run program that helps employees during crises: a fire, a serious illness, an accident. The only resource the hospital provides is a full-time employee who manages the program. Through voluntary payroll deductions from employees and some fund-raisers, the society collects about $125,000 a year. Employees also contribute vacation and sick time for those who really need it.

The Job

People need to be in the right job, one they like and that motivates them to excel. Ideally, your employees should always be able to answer yes to the three questions central to happiness on the job: Do I love what I do? Do I do it well? Can you pay me for it? Three yes answers usually indicate a good relationship with the job.

It's always better to pay people for what they love to do rather than for what they hate to do. A person who loves his or her job will look for opportunities to expand it, to improve processes, and to be more innovative. If the job is truly a dead-end, look at ways to feed the other five relationships and to focus on how the work itself is done, from offering more job flexibility to helping the job fit more easily into the work-life equation.

Sallie Mae connects its rank-and-file employees to their jobs by offering them approximately half of the stock options it grants as a corporation. "It's a tremendous commitment," Reich says. "It really says a lot about how much we value them." Sallie Mae stock has done extremely well over the years—a five-year average annualized total return of 26 percent. Reich notes that hourly employees who kept the options offered to them since 1997 have earned an additional $250,000. "These stock options have changed their lives in a real way that they can't imagine with any other company. It's also bolstered the good relations between management and our workforce."

The Career

People want to move forward and grow. Unfortunately, though, when it comes to careers, most of us are left to our own devices. Organizations may offer training programs. But more often, they pay the most attention to people's careers after a layoff or downsizing—patching the pain with outplacement services. What a difference it would make if just 10 percent of the energy put into outplacement were directed toward inplacement—nurturing careers while people are still with the organization!

With an intentional focus from management, people could gain additional skills that would help the organization perform. When you meet regularly with your people, add career to the agenda, talking about where they want to go next and what they want to do. How do you leverage their experience to help them get there?

An IT specialist at Revlon expressed an interest in training. For one day a week, her supervisor let her serve in HR, where she learned how to be an effective trainer. When a training job opened, she applied and got it. Imagine how this increased her loyalty to the organization! And Revlon got to see her in action before offering the position.

At its Barkdale facility, W. L. Gore started an internship program that lets people work 10 percent of the workweek in any other department. The goal is to build new skills and advance careers so that employees are more marketable in finding their next jobs inside the company. If you're going to prepare people for new jobs, why not make it simple for them to find something where they are?

Cross-training and internship programs help people manage their careers as they go—and, ultimately, keep people in the organization by sending the message, You don't have to jump from company to company to get ahead; you can jump and get ahead here. It's a very different model from what most companies use. And it yields an enduring benefit for the company, which gets to try out candidates for a job before hiring them.

Land's End has an excellent program that lets employees try out a new job before committing to it. This "try before you buy" program, modeled after the excellent garments they sell online, lets each employee try out a new job for up to six months before accepting it full-time. The result? The vast majority of jobs at Land's End are filled with internal candidates. This results in reduced hiring costs and enhanced loyalty from employees.

Customers

Everyone in the organization needs to be connected to the customer. Current business models have been built on organizations that didn't have to compete aggressively to stay in business. Over the past 50 years, we've seen companies spring up and profit because each was the only show in town. Now, with advanced technology and the new global economy, organizations are competing not just with local competitors but with competitors around the world.

Relentless competition requires rethinking how people become connected to the customer. It asks organizations to connect people in a way that's different from anything they've ever done before, developing faster relationships with their customers and determining exactly which experiences customers are willing to pay for.

In most organizations, the sales team is very connected to the customer, but other departments are in the dark. Every person in the organization needs to have some connection to the customer. Even if employees don't have day-to-day customer contact, they need to understand who customers are and what those customers are buying.

If your business produces women's hair care products, every employee needs to know what women today want for their hair. Put a face on the product: Who is the customer? What is she buying? What does she say when she buys one of your products? This face needs to be incorporated into every part of the organization, from how you hire to how you coach. Paint the picture of the customer, and give people a reason to connect. Determine what the customer needs, incorporate it into the Destination, and define each person's contribution to it. This will drive raises, bonuses, and feedback—and will naturally tease out what your customers want.

Most organizations set up their systems to do what works for them internally, not what works for the customer. A case in point is the airline policy on Saturday night stays. This policy was designed to fill seats with leisure travelers during downtimes: weekends. Unfortunately, the policy punishes business travelers, their most profitable customers, who end up staying over a weekend in order to save precious company dollars. This policy may have worked for the airlines but certainly did not work for customers.

Our bet is that the people who made those decisions were sitting in an office somewhere, far removed from the frontline agents who know what customers want. It's telling that the legacy airlines that instituted this business model all are or have been in bankruptcy recently, while the airlines that don't participate— JetBlue and Southwest—are profitable. Your organization must be in touch with those nuances, rules, and policies that no longer make any sense for your organization or for your customers.

To your customers, it is your employees and your ways of doing business that shape the brand of your organization. Sure, advertising helps, but the real depth that comes from consistent high-quality products and services cannot be duplicated in any form of advertisement. From our perspective, everyone's title in an organization should be either Profit Enhancement Specialist or Customer Advocacy Specialist. If that were the case, imagine what a different experience the organization and the customer would have!

Onboarding: The Critical Foundation

The first days on the job are critical. In those days, the new hire should be able to give affirmative answers to several key questions. From the personal side: Were they ready for me? Did I make the best choice for me, my career, and my family? Is my job important here? Will they care about me? From the business side: Do I know what is expected of me? Do I understand how my responsibilities align with the company's overall goals?

If an employee can't answer these questions positively in the first week, he or she will begin to disconnect from the organization, giving up on those initial hopes and dreams of success.

The seeds of the six key relationships, discussed earlier, are planted during the first weeks on the job, beginning with a robust onboarding program that includes the steps shown in Figure 1. Starting at the bottom of the pyramid's foundation, they are:

- **Taking care of basics.** Before new hires can begin to connect to the business, they need to be assured that their financial and health needs will be met. So get the paperwork out of the way, answer all the questions about insurance and benefits, and show new hires up front that your organization has given thought to their arrival by planning out their time and understanding their needs.

  We attended an orientation program for a drugstore that wanted to expand its connection with newly hired employees. While the store's orientation program was good, it did not include lunch for the new hires. The site did not have a cafeteria, and the closest eating place was not within walking distance. New hires were left to fend for themselves. Throughout the orientation program, they drove in small groups to a local fast-food restaurant, where they complained about how cheap the company was for not providing them with a meal. This was another missed opportunity to build relationships over a common occurrence in most of our lives—lunch.

As it turned out, the company had a policy against providing lunches. But no one thought through the implications for new hires. That first chance to connect became an immediate disconnect.

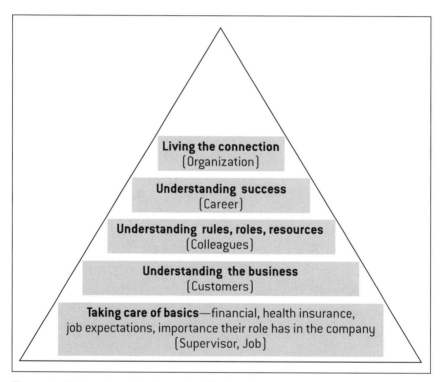

Figure 1. Connecting People to the Business
Source: ModernThink Consulting LLC, 2006

- **Understanding the business.** New hires need to understand the tactical side of how the organization makes money or fulfills its promises to customers. This might include an overview of the brand, market position, product or service list, business strategy, what distinguishes it from competitors, and an overall review of the entire organization and how the various parts work together. Make sure new hires clearly understand the role your organization plays in its industry, with competitors, and in the world at large. This is also the time to introduce your new employees to your customers or at least provide information about your customers, including who they are, what their buying habits are, and what your philosophy is in serving them.

- **Understanding rules, roles, and resources.** New hires need to understand how what they do will drive the organization toward leaders' carefully crafted Destinations. While understanding the Destination is critical, you also need to share the history of how you chose that Destination, so that you can get support and generate excitement about arriving there. Help new hires begin the process of knowing who's who, what's what, and who and what in the organization will help them perform the jobs they were hired to do.

- **Understanding success.** In this step, newly hired employees begin to see how they fit in and what's really expected of them in reaching the organization's Destination. Answer key questions they may have about performance, such as the following:

  - Who will celebrate with me when I succeed?
  - What are the consequences if I don't do well?
  - What are the rewards if I do?

- What kind of coaching and feedback can I expect?
- Can I really speak up?
- What does a win look like for me, for my team, and for my organization?

It's here that people begin to bring their full selves to the organization. They start sharing their thoughts and ideas. Any time people can freely offer their thoughts, they're one step closer to connecting with the organization.

- **Living the connection.** If your organization has succeeded in the first four steps of connection, you've built a strong foundation for the fifth step. New hires, no longer new, will begin to live the connection, doing whatever it takes to move the business ahead and toward the Destinations. They will continue to stay connected through the ongoing delivery of their contributions and the deepening of critical workplace relationships. The ultimate goal is to turn employees into fans of the organization. Fans believe in the organization and advocate for it wherever they go, selling and recruiting at every opportunity.

The goal, of course, is to connect people to your organization and keep them connected. Just remember, connecting employees to your business starts well before they join. Some organizations have used the interview process to create fans and future customers. For example, one of Coca-Cola's hiring practices is to make sure that anyone interviewed, whether hired or not, leaves the interview wanting to drink another Coke. How about your organization? Does your hiring process turn everyone who interviews with you into a new or more loyal customer?

> >> *Is the recruiting process set up to also enhance the image and sales of your product or service, or just to hire the new person?*

Orientation programs must have a defined and meaningful purpose, beyond processing paperwork and forms. The most effective orientation programs make new hires feel immediately cared for—and start the process of connecting them to the business. You get this opportunity just once! And it's much easier and faster to connect employees to the organization from the start than to try reconnecting them later.

Con-way's orientation program goes a long way in establishing the connection with employees. New employees go to their company headquarters where an intensive get-to-know-your-company program begins.

Often as many as 90 employees attend and participate in presentations and discussions with company executives. "The president talks about company structure and personnel policies. The VP of sales talks about marketing and the benefits and solutions provided by our products and services. The controller explains where our revenue goes, how our cost structure is set up, and how our bonus plan works. The directors of safety and operations help them understand how we provide service to our customers," says Pat Jannausch. At lunchtime, employees are served in the cafeteria by the leaders they just met at orientation. "Our executives are often found behind the counter, doling out mashed potatoes," Jannausch explains. "Then they join the new employees for lunch to continue the conversation."

Five years after the orientation, at one Con-way company these same employees return to hear again from executives who update them on the challenges, successes, and advances of the organization and industry over the past five years. The company calls this program You Ensure Success, or YES. "Here, employees have a chance to say yes again to Con-way," Jannausch says. "They're reinformed and reacknowledged as contributing members in Con-way's success and have the opportunity to rededicate to the company."

JetBlue Airways also has an outstanding orientation program that we had the joy of participating in. We walked into a room of about 80 people in the company's training center, located in Forest Hills, New York. It set the tone for an instant connection to the business. Music was playing, everyone was shaking hands and asking which crew team they were joining. Models of the JetBlue planes, the Airbus A320 and the Embraer 190, were on each side of the room. People were having a good time and being themselves. There was excitement about who's who and what's what and where everyone is going. Something about being there made you want to contribute immediately. Something just connected you to everyone in the room. Blue seemed to be the last thing anyone was feeling!

JetBlue's values were displayed across the front of the room. A quote on the wall said, "The choice for greatness is an act of serving others." It's from Captain Mike Barger, VP and chief learning officer. Another, from Chris Collins, JetBlue's flight operations manager, said, "The measure of success is not whether you have a problem to deal with, but whether it is the same problem you had last year." Also on the back wall, a huge painting displayed JetBlue's ultimate Destination: "To make the world a better place, one flight at a time." These thoughts framed the introduction for new employees.

Leaders asked new hires to talk about a flight they really loved. Some said they liked it when the captain spoke to them. Others agreed they enjoyed it when they felt involved and informed. Some recalled a flight that was smooth. Then, the group was asked what they liked about JetBlue flights. They reaffirmed a lot of the same points—along with saying that they liked the TVs. And they liked that when things went badly, from missed luggage to bad weather, the JetBlue crew was so responsive and gave out coupons and gifts. One new hire yelled out, "That's the most amazing thing!"

New crew members introduced themselves with an excitement usually reserved for spirited sports events. The energy in the room could not have been a stronger indication and validation of the superior hiring practices of JetBlue's Department of People. As guests, we were also asked to introduce ourselves. When our turn came, we stood up and shared our names and explained that while we were only JetBlue guests for the day, after hearing all the excitement in the room, we wished we were joining them, too. To which one new hire quipped, "Good luck. It's taken me three years to get in here!"

>> *How does your organization's onboarding program connect new hires to the business?*

Celebrating and Appreciating

Most people want to succeed, and they love to have their accomplishments celebrated through some form of acknowledgment. If you show them how they're being successful, they'll strive to be even more successful. Behavior is repeated when it gets attention. And if you ignore people's efforts, you risk reducing morale and productivity.

Recognition may be as simple as saying, "You're doing a good job" or "We couldn't have done this without you." It could be a handwritten thank-you note, with a copy for the files. Or it could be having an informal team meeting or a formal recognition ceremony to acknowledge people's unique contributions. A Wichita State University study finds the top two meaningful workforce incentives are personal thanks and a written thank-you from a manager.

Positive recognition encourages people to contribute more and give their discretionary energy—the extra effort that invariably leads to bigger profits. It's also a great way to reinforce company values and promote successful teaming.

Southwest holds frequent company gatherings to inspire and rally employees. On any given day, there are multiple celebrations at this airline known for its fun culture. There might be a surprise unveiling in the headquarters for the unsung heros— those who work behind the scenes to make the airline run so well. Acknowledgment and thanks are always the foundation of these events, celebrating people for delivering on the promise with their commitment and contributions.

Data Return has quarterly employee meetings where awards are given out as a way of acknowledging people who are living the company's Guiding Principles. "When you watch the managers giving these awards, you realize how much they understand the Guiding Principles and are using them to reinforce positive behaviors," says Chief Learning Officer Rand Stagen.

At Alston & Bird, the managing partner of the Atlanta office holds a company meeting at the end of each month. "In most law firms, these kinds of meetings would be for attorneys only," says Chief Human Resources Officer Cathy Benton. "At A&B, anyone can come. Our attorneys talk about the business of the firm and recognize every person who worked on each deal, from partners and associates to paralegal secretaries—even the people who set up the conference room. Everybody is acknowledged for being part of the team."

Sometimes, employers make gestures of appreciation that are meant to be generous—but they send the wrong message. We heard the story of an "appreciation lunch" for staff assistants in a Fortune 500 company. Assistants received formal invitations to an hour-and-a-half lunch at a pricey restaurant—at their own expense—intended to honor their contributions. Travel time to and from the restaurant was exactly half an hour. The company showcased the half-hour beyond the usual lunch hour as its "gift." That's the kind of appreciation we might be better off without!

Solid Returns, Greed, and Giving Back

Somewhere along the continuum of success, profit takes a gigantic leap and moves from solid returns to greed. We believe every company will find its own line and should be able to answer the question "If profit is your only goal, then how much profit is enough?"

Is there such a thing as too much profit? When profit is sought regardless of the carnage left behind, it's usually not profit. It's greed. Don't get us wrong. We think wealth accumulation is a great goal for businesses. Yet, step even one inch into greed, and everything becomes disconnected. Why? Leaders can't sustain profit as the Destination, because it lacks the depth and meaning that engages employees. Plus, profitability is an essential element of business, but not the goal, as it is difficult to sustain when the economy swings. This is especially true, of course, in an economic downturn. Profit goals are fine in hot economies, but they are disastrous in weak economies because you've prepared your organization only to make money, not to adapt when you're not making money. What sustains a business, regardless of what's happening outside, is the right culture. We've found that leading businesses practice responsible economic growth— using part of their profits not only to advance their people and the industry but also to give back to the community.

Who wants to make a difference in the world? Who doesn't! Organizations that open up opportunities for their employees to do something good for others are fulfilling a basic need for their people—and for the world. In fact, people may be so busy working that they aren't able to contribute time to charitable causes except for a day or two during the year-end holidays. Employees therefore look to their employers to help them find ways to give back to the community or the world at large. This type of activity gives employees the chance to provide for others and builds compelling workplaces. Selfless acts are meaningful, and the more you can help employees connect to their sense of humanity, the more likely they are to stay closely connected to your organization. Many companies have initiatives that do this.

Medtronic, a leading medical technology company, builds heart valves and other products that save lives. As a way of connecting employees to the bigger picture, the company invites people who use their products to come in and talk about the difference these products have made in their quality of life. The stories are often very touching and inspire employees to give more in their work.

Timberland has made community service an integral part of its strategy and brand identity. The company realized it couldn't afford to release an employee for lengthy service projects, say, those lasting several months. In devising a program that would support the community but not hurt the company financially, leaders came up with a plan that would allow an employee to take, for example, six months off to help out with Habitat for Humanity, as long as the volunteer's team is willing and able to work extra hours to cover that person's time. The team decides. It's a program that creates lasting connections—from employees to Timberland, from Timberland to the community, and from the community to Timberland employees. Thus, you can not only help make Timberland products that serve the world but also use the Timberland experience to change the world, one project at a time!

Sallie Mae is one of *BusinessWeek*'s Top Corporate Philanthropists and one of the 15 top cash givers among companies nationwide. It set up a charitable organization, The Sallie Mae Fund, to support initiatives that help open doors to higher education. Annual giving programs exceed $12 million. The fund also encourages employee volunteerism and service in the communities where Sallie Mae employees live and work. Suddenly, at

Sallie Mae, you can go from processing education loans to helping educate others!

Perkins Coie has an extensive community program for attorneys and staff. Projects range from setting up apartments at a homeless shelter to taking on pro bono cases. Pro bono time has reached as much as 27,000 hours a year, or an estimated $8 million of donated work, according to Darrin Emerick, chief personnel officer.

Giving of yourself, your talents, and your time is a wonderful reminder of what you have, and what better place to be reminded of that than where you work? Giving to those in need is more than a smart business decision. It's the right thing to do—not just for the people or the community you're helping, but also for the employees and the organization. It models a solid value: Focus more on what you can give and less on what you can get.

People as People First

People are more than employees. They're whole persons, always in the process of developing. They need to know they can bring all that they are to their organizations, not just the employee part.

Many managers believe people can simply leave their personal lives at home when they're working. Not true! And why should they? We certainly expect employees to take work home with them. Why wouldn't we expect them to bring home to work?

As with everything in life, feelings drive performance. If you're worried about finding child care, or taking care of an ailing parent, or buying a new home, the chances of doing your best work are minimized. It's like the hiring process: We get the best of the individual in the interview, yet the whole person shows up on the first day. Changing how we think of employees —seeing them as people—does indeed take a shift in focus. MBA programs rarely teach anyone to see past the employee and certainly do not advocate an aggressive stance on seeing the whole person. What a missed opportunity!

Leaders need to know what motivates each whole person on their teams. They start out by knowing who the person is and then understanding that individual's needs. When managers realize that the needs of a human being are the same inside the workplace as they are outside the workplace, they also tend to get a more robust workplace. Most people need the same basic things: being included, being recognized, feeling competent, not feeling embarrassed, being loved. Why would these things change just because they're at work?

A bank in the Midwest had a significant problem with its call center productivity and retention. As is typically the case in call centers, this one was experiencing alarming turnover. In trying to build a better connection with employees, management asked all call center employees to put together personal profiles filled with information about themselves as people. Based on the profile results, managers began scheduling people with similar interests on the same shift. They did this intentionally, so that during breaks and lunches, which were extended three times a week, each employee could participate in a scheduled activity.

One shift had people who loved sports. They played volleyball together. Another had people who were single parents. They talked through single-parent issues. Yet another had a group of crossword puzzle devotees who compared new words and participated in timed races for puzzle championships. The bank's ability to see past the employee and into the whole person opened up new and better ways of doing business.

This bank would never have thought of offering this new program had leaders not realized that their call center people were disconnected from the organization. Putting together people with shared interests brought an enormous return to call center team members, the bank, and customers. It also strengthened the employee-employer connection. The results of this new way of thinking were lauded throughout the bank and adopted systemwide in all call center locations. Productivity, as measured by the bank, improved tremendously, turnover was dramatically reduced, and the job itself was made easier because people could relieve their stress by having fun on every shift.

> **>> How does your work environment contribute to individual success or failure?**

Wegmans food markets, *Fortune*'s top company to work for in America in 2005, found an innovative way to connect to a key part of its workforce—teens from 16 to 18 years old. Concerned that the average turnover rate for this group was much higher than it wanted, the company took a look at how it could best relate to the teens as people, not just as employees. Leaders asked themselves a critical question: "What do we have in common with employees who are 16 to 18 years old?" The list was relatively short. Then they asked the right question: "What do we have in common with *people* who are 16 to 18 years old?"

They found the answer in proms! All prom-bound employees were invited to stop by the store on the night of the prom to have their pictures taken and receive the good wishes of store employees who cheered them on. Then, when the students arrived at the prom, they enjoyed refreshments donated by their Wegmans store. The prom tie-in not only has reduced teen turnover but has built employee loyalty in a specific group of employees—teenagers, whose average tenure in most organizations is less than three months. Wegmans also maintains its close relationship with teen employees by offering numerous college scholarship programs. These teens go off to college, they often return on school breaks to work at Wegmans, and when they graduate, where do you think they apply for work? And where do you think they shop?

Perkins Coie brings people together informally through its brown-bag lunch seminars. Discussion topics cover anything employees think is important, from how to save money to how to communicate tragedy to children, the subject of a series of brown-bag lunches after 9/11. Instead of focusing only on the needs of the business, these lunches blend life needs and work issues—a further indication that employees are truly members of a larger "family."

> *"A lot of organizations believe you leave the family behind when you come to work. That's not realistic."*
>
> —Cathy Benton, Chief Human Resources Officer, Alston & Bird

Alston & Bird honors families with a children's art wall in each of its five offices, showcasing the latest creations of employees' children. "Family is really important to us," says Cathy Benton, chief people officer. The art walls are just one example of the joy people feel in coming to work every day at A&B. "Our people really like what they do," Benton says. "They feel challenged and creative, and they share a special camaraderie."

Pathway #3: Know Who You Really Are

We've found that most organizations know *what* they are, but not always *who* they are. Knowing who you are comes down to defining your culture—and building your business around that collective identity.

Culture isn't something that can be described in a manual. It isn't passed on by edict. It has fuzzy boundaries, because it's made up of human beings. But if you don't deliberately define your culture, your culture will define itself by what people bring to your organization—from leadership behaviors, to communication styles, to what and how people celebrate.

"Culture," says Rand Stagen, Data Return's CLO, "is like that story of the sculptor who was asked, 'How did you create that beautiful piece of artwork?' He answered, 'It was always there. I just chipped away at the rock.'"

> *"Culture is art. It's abstract, intangible,*
> *and intuitive. You have to feel it."*
> —Rand Stagen, CLO, Data Return

"You can't not have a culture," says Mike Barger, VP and chief learning officer at JetBlue. "A culture will grow, with or without you. It's up to the leadership to define and direct it."

Barger admits it's a lot easier to start out with a clean slate and build a culture than to turn a culture around later on. One of JetBlue's top priorities has been to set a cultural business vision that supports its business plan. While margins, costs, revenues, and marketing opportunities are part of the business plan, the company has also focused intensely on the people experience. Leaders realized they had to create something that would lure not only new customers but also new "crew members"—JetBlue's term for its employees. When asked for the "secret sauce recipe" for JetBlue, Barger suggests that it takes creating a culture where people are committed to serving the company and the customers—and feel they're being well served, too.

SC Johnson has defined who it is through four cultural constants. First, as touted in every television commercial, it's a family company. Employees have an unwavering commitment and loyalty to the Johnson family, derived from the same unwavering commitment and loyalty the family has to its employees and its customers.

Second, SCJ takes a people-first, profits-second approach. The company is a highly engaged and competitive organization that has managed to compete with organizations 10 times its size and still maintain the first- or second-place market position for the product categories in which it competes worldwide.

Third, SCJ has an organizational document called "This We Believe." It's the company's "moral compass—the soul of SC Johnson," says Kelly Semrau, vice president of global public affairs and communication. "Sam Johnson knew he had something special in his company and wanted to make sure it endured," she explains. "This document is a map for how we will be. It talks about mutual respect, honesty, and how we're all here to make the world better in the communities in which we operate." The document has existed for nearly 40 years. You may hear language like this at SCJ: "This doesn't quite feel right. This just doesn't feel like 'This We Believe.'" The document truly guides the company's operations worldwide and serves as an internal guide to how people are to treat one another as well as anyone who deals with the company.

Fourth, everyone at SCJ, from CEO to line worker, feels the need to leave a legacy. A legacy may be large or small. It may be that the line manager runs the best line possible or has reduced production time by a nanosecond. It could be making a distinct contribution to the culture. But it indeed is a legacy.

Is this a competitive advantage? Absolutely. All the people at SC Johnson know they can and should be looking to leave a legacy. This has enabled the company to enjoy enormous innovativeness as people focus more on giving than on getting. In a world so focused on "what's in it for me?" SC Johnson has managed to keep to a simpler philosophy of "what can I do for you?" The company has amassed an unusually rich culture that enables its people to find their joy in working at a family company—one that prides itself on being more innovative, productive, and able to provide superior products by intentionally shaping a unique workplace experience.

Hiring for Who You Are

Organizational culture comes with a menu of descriptions: Customer-focused. Innovative. Aggressive. Flexible. Laid-back. Risk-taking. Family-friendly. It's OK to be whoever you are as an organization. It's OK, for example, to have an intense, highly driven, whatever-it-takes culture. Just know it—and sell it during the hiring process, so that the top talent you bring in will do well in the work environment you offer. By painting an accurate picture of your culture, you give the candidate the choice to buy in or opt out.

What is top talent? Only individual organizations can answer that question because top talent is relative to the company. Not every superstar at another company will be a superstar in your organization. You must factor in your culture, mission, Destinations, vision, and values, as all of these affect a person's ability to do his or her best work. If any of these factors doesn't resonate for employees, it can cause an immediate disconnect for the very people you're counting on to create additional business. We have known amazingly gifted individuals who have floundered when put into the wrong company because they simply couldn't make things happen in that particular environment.

We must view top talent through the lens of the organization's culture. It's long been suggested that people are the most important asset in an organization. That's not entirely true. It's actually the *right* people, those who can maximize contributions, who are the most important asset. We don't believe in general that there are bad employees in organizations, yet we do believe that there are many good people in the wrong jobs or at the wrong time in their lives to help their organization perform. A top-talent manager from Microsoft might not be the same top talent needed at Disney or Procter & Gamble. Top talents are only top talent when they can excel and get things done in your organization and for your customers.

>> *What type of employees do their best work inside your organization?*

Hiring the best is conditional on knowing who you are as an organization.

Those you hire who can do well inside your particular culture · will be more apt to stay longer, understand the expectations more clearly, and decide for themselves how to spend their time growing the business. They will also help perpetuate the culture and strengthen the organization's efforts.

Alston & Bird looks for people who value teamwork, have a stellar work ethic, produce quality work, and are committed to service excellence. The firm scrupulously screens for these non-negotiable characteristics in its interviewing and hiring processes.

"We hire tough and manage easy."

—Cathy Benton, Chief Human Resources Officer, Alston & Bird

Sallie Mae looks for people who are performance driven. "No matter what you do at our company, from working in the mailroom to serving as an executive leader, we have very high expectations for every single employee," says Joni Reich, senior vice president of administration. "Our philosophy is, setting high expectations brings out the best in people, and if someone isn't comfortable with always striving to be the best, then maybe this isn't the best place for them to work."

Patience is a key quality that Corning seeks in its employees. "Our inventions can take years—decades, even—to get to market. It's rarely instant gratification," notes Anne Kenlon, corporate communications. "We look for people who can take a long-term strategic view of where we're going as a company and where they're going in their own careers."

The Container Store, a national retail chain, has purposefully created a culture that stands out from those of other retailers. Company founders Garrett Boone and Kip Tindell use an unusual word to describe their culture: yummy. They're extremely choosy about whom they hire because they recognize that one mistake could erode the unique culture they've worked so hard to build.

What's so yummy about the Container Store? The company pays its workers generously, 50 to 100 percent more than the retail industry average, believing that one great worker is three times more productive than "just a good one," so it makes sense to pay larger salaries to fewer workers. The Container Store also invests heavily in training to educate new workers and immerse them in the corporate culture. New full-time employees receive 235 hours of training, compared to the industry average of 7 hours.

SAS Institute also hires directly for the culture it has built. "If your goal is to work where you can climb the corporate ladder, it's a different ladder here from the one you learned about in business school," says John Dornan, manager of corporate public relations. "If you come here with the traditional model in mind, it'll drive you nuts. Considering the tenure of people who are here, the climb to the top could take 20 years. You'll be recognized and well paid, but you won't be moving rapidly to a managerial or executive career track. That's not who we are."

SAS doesn't use temps or contractors because it hires for the long term. Although the initial process may be lengthy, the company finds that it's worth it to focus on hiring the right fit and avoid paying the price later on. As a result, voluntary turnover at SAS is about 3 percent. Most who leave do so in the first few months. This low turnover rate saves the company an estimated $75 million a year.

"Data Return filters all recruiting and hiring through our core ideology," explains CEO Sunny Vanderbeck. "Eventually our competitors will have equivalent technology and systems," he says, adding that "the key differentiator is how our clients experience our people and culture—the intangible essence that we call Mojo."

> *"What can't be replicated is our Mojo—the experience*
> *our clients have in working with our team."*
> —Sunny Vanderbeck, CEO, Data Return

If an organization does its work, then, seeking to understand who it is and what it does and doesn't stand for, it has a great opportunity to leverage this information in virtually every interaction in the organization, internally and externally. If you're unsure of who your company is, we recommend you try Exercise 1.

Pathway #4: Cultivate Commitment, Not Compliance

Policies and processes can be used either to rule people or to support people. The power in an organization is not in forcing people to do what's right. It's in giving them the ability to choose what's right. "Because it's policy" should never be the reason for doing things. Instead, the thinking behind the policy and how it benefits the organization need to be explained. The goal is to cultivate commitment, not compliance. What would happen if you eliminated some of your policies from your organization? We believe you might see significant behavioral changes, for the good of the business!

Some would insist that rules are essential guideposts, yet does the rule in and of itself eliminate undesired behavior? Of course not. The rule only matters when people don't follow it. We're not

WHO ARE WE?

Think about your company as you answer each of the following questions:

1. I would describe our organization in the following 10 words:

2. People who work here tend to be:

3. Customers love the fact that, internally, we:

4. When all is said and done, this place exudes:

5. Leaders here are usually:

6. The most compelling reason to work here is:

7. The best way to succeed here is to have these traits:

8. The type of employee who always fails in our organization is:

9. We think of ourselves as:

10. When we want to celebrate good work, we usually:

suggesting that you throw out your policy manuals just yet. We want you to work up to it, though.

Here's an example of two approaches to a policy. Restaurant A serves a lunch special with potato chips. Managers tell the waitstaff that there is a no-substitutions policy. No exceptions. A customer has a strong craving for French fries, but when she requests fries with the lunch special, the server tells her no. She asks why, and the server says there's a no-substitutions policy. The customer feels slighted by the server, leaves a small tip, and never returns. Restaurant B also serves a lunch special with chips. Instead of handing down a policy, managers explain to the servers that serving chips helps keep the cost down so that the restaurant can offer the special price. A customer really wants fries, and the server explains that really they're more expensive to prepare than chips but, for an extra dollar to cover the difference, the restaurant will gladly serve her fries. As a result, the customer is happy, and the restaurant benefits from a larger sale.

When the server offers a reason for the rule, we feel included and can be more understanding. But saying something is so just because it's the rule doesn't work. Cultivate commitment from employees and customers by involving them in discussion about the thinking behind the rule and why it makes sense for your business.

Southwest Airlines got rid of its policy book and replaced it with Guidelines for Leaders, which is one-fourth the size of the previous manual. Rather than providing absolute rules, it offers guidelines on what to consider in a variety of employee situations, which empowers leaders to make decisions that make sense for the situation.

East Alabama Medical Center has policies, but they're overridden if they conflict with what's best for employees in specific situations.

*"We discourage our people from just quoting policy.
What's most important is doing the right thing."*

—Terry Andrus, CEO, East Alabama Medical Center

Con-way has adopted a Corporate Constitution built on four core values: Safety, Integrity, Commitment, and Excellence. Every September, at Con-way locations around the country, employees are asked to sign a copy of the Corporate Constitution, reaffirming their devotion to these values. Constitution-signing is accompanied by a "Keeping the Dream Alive" celebration. The company has even published two books of stories, submitted by employees, that illustrate values-driven behavior, both on and off the job.

SC Johnson doesn't rely on rules-based decision-making. It relies instead on "This We Believe" decision-making, says Kelly Semrau, referring to the 40-year-old document that guides employee behavior. "You have to feel absolutely comfortable with ambiguity here, because our decision-making is so unique. You have to approach the business from an intellectual and emotional basis, because to leave a legacy, you need to be connected to the business in both these ways."

Every organization will face tough times. W. L. Gore & Associates has weathered the changes throughout the years by adapting its practices but holding strong to its core values, which have not changed since the day the company opened its doors.

Rather than using traditional policy manuals to communicate its preferences on behavior, Gore uses four simple, yet highly effective, principles to guide its associates:

- **Fairness Principle.** Everyone will try to be fair. Everyone will sincerely strive to be fair with one another, our suppliers, our customers, and all persons with whom we carry out transactions.

- **Freedom Principle.** Everyone will allow, help, and encourage other Associates to grow in knowledge, skill, scope of responsibility, and range of activities.

- **Commitment Principle.** Everyone will make his or her own commitments—and keep them.

- **Waterline Principle.** Everyone will consult with other Associates before taking actions that might be "below the waterline" and cause serious damage to the Enterprise.

According to W. L. Gore CEO Terri Kelly, principles help guide associates to make better decisions. Ultimately, she says, it comes down to exercising good judgment, which can never be replaced by a long, detailed policy manual. The principles also inform how associates relate to one another and to customers. It's no accident that customers readily build and leverage their personal relationships with Gore associates.

> **>> How are you encouraging your people to choose what's right?**

Influence, Not Power

All too often, leaders try to increase their power by solving all problems themselves or spotlighting their own successes over those of their teams. A better choice is to be an information seeker and people supporter who actively influences by seeking and listening to the input of others.

Starbucks CEO Jim Donnell is a master at making people feel valued. When he comes into his office every day, he immediately makes 10 phone calls to randomly selected stores. He introduces himself to whoever answers the phone and asks how things are going. That's influence!

"Our leaders are not truly recognized as leaders until their team embraces their leadership."

—Terri Kelly, CEO, W. L. Gore & Associates, Inc.

Leaders also need to know how to inspire those who follow. You may be hired at W. L. Gore with an official "commitment" (Gore's word for a job) to lead a team, but you're not the leader right away. You have to earn the right, and that takes time, relationship development, and careful execution.

W. L. Gore calls this "followership." CEO Terri Kelly says, "Here, leaders who cannot establish followership, as confirmed by those they lead, are not kept in their leadership roles."

>> *Do leaders in your organization look for power or for influence?*

Pathway #5: Create an Equitable Experience for Your People

Equity is a powerful thing. It's a basic human need to feel that we've been treated fairly. Why do you think children complain, "Mom, he has a bigger piece of cake than I do!"? Why do we agree to split things 50/50 or take out the garbage because someone else took it out last time? Why do we get upset when someone cuts ahead of us in line after we've been waiting for an hour? It's because we have a basic sense of fairness.

When employees believe they are being treated unfairly, they have a major reason to disconnect from their organization and, in the end, to leave it. Perceptions of fairness are often based on quick interactions that many involved don't realize are considered unfair. Plus, the acceptable ratio of fairness to unfairness is grossly off-scale: You could have a hundred fair things going for you, but when just one unfair issue arises you suddenly have major problems. At our core, we believe that fairness is our right, and we believe supervisors and organizations are no exception.

Being or feeling treated unfairly brings out the absolute worst in everyone. A woman was seen leaving the movie theater with her coat pockets bulging with napkins. She was asked, "What's going on with the napkins?" "I paid $13.75 for this popcorn and soda," she said. "I'm getting my money's worth!"

That's how it can be in the workplace. When people perceive unfairness at work, they can retaliate in all sorts of ways. They take things—and not just things from the supply closet. They withhold ideas, perspectives, service, and communication. They don't give their best performance. They see opportunities and don't act on or share them. That withholding costs the organization at every level.

> > *How does your organization define fairness for your people, your vendors, and your customers?*

Scott was giving a speech to the top 250 officers of a multinational company. The room was set up classroom style. To the left of the podium, Scott noticed a lot of blue. During one of the breaks, he walked over to see what the blue was and found rows of Dasani brand water bottles. People in the first two rows had their own bottles of nicely chilled Dasani. As Scott looked around the room, he noticed that other people had pitchers of tap water and concluded that the hotel must have run out of Dasani.

Then he noticed that the chairs were different in the first two rows. They had much thicker cushions than the chairs in the other rows. When the break was over, he noticed that all the people who took seats in the first row had name badges with their first and last names. The badges of the other 220 people had first names only. All of a sudden, it dawned on him that these first two rows were for the executive team. And everybody else in the room, although an officer, was not a member of the executive team. Ironically, Scott was talking about the issue of minimizing status differences and creating an equitable and fair workplace.

This story, which has come to be known as "The Dasani Water Story," is an illustration of unnecessary status differences in organizations. The intended message was that the people in the first two rows were important (as if having a bigger title and a higher salary weren't enough). But the message received was that the people in the other rows were unimportant! The questions posed to the group afterward were "Why can't we all have bottled water or all have pitchers?" And "Why do some people deserve thicker cushions than others?"

We worked with one organization that closely monitored arrival times for hourly workers. If they were late, they were disciplined, without exception. Yet, managers were allowed to stroll in whenever they pleased. While most managers arrived early, there were enough who didn't that the hourly people began to complain. It's OK to have a policy of starting on time, but why wouldn't you make this effective for everyone, and cultivate it as a commitment instead of a rule?

We run into policies like this every day. Most of us just hope we're on the better end of the policy, in this case, on the management side. We worked with one manager who felt that the number of hours employees worked was equivalent to their loyalty to the organization and their worth as employees. As a result of this manager's attitude, employees would race in every morning to beat the manager into the office only to sneak out later to do errands or go to the gym. Many who came in early were asked to turn on the lights in the offices of co-workers so it would appear that those co-workers were already there. Talk about dysfunction! Whenever you send a message about what's valued beyond contributions, you're most likely also sending a message that people are treated differently according to status.

Another client had a wonderful holiday celebration each year, with great food, drinks, and a small gift for each employee. The problem was, however, that if you were an hourly employee, you went to one party, and if you were a manager, you went to another. Size was given as the reason for the two parties, but the division into hourly and managerial employees sent a very different message. If size was indeed the concern, perhaps it would have been better to break down the population by department, or randomly by last name, instead.

SAS Institute has made a practice of fairness since its founding in 1976. "From landscape and cafeteria workers to the CEO, everybody here gets the same profit sharing, health plan, and access to benefits," says Jeff Chambers, vice president of human resources.

W. L. Gore has mastered the fairness principle with everyone inside, and outside, the organization. Being fair with employees, as well as with vendors and anyone with whom the company interacts, is a cornerstone of Gore culture. Gore also recognizes that fairness does not mean treating everyone the same but means opening different opportunities based on each associate's capabilities.

Gore has removed the traditional role of supervisor, providing instead sponsors who serve as coaches, not bosses. Their role is to make sure employees maximize their contributions. Compensation is based on team members' assessment of each individual's contribution to the business.

Each year team members meet to rank each person's contribution to the enterprise, defined by "impact times effectiveness."

Every team member comments and has equal input. An individual may appear on multiple lists, depending on the teams he or she has worked with. The final rank order determines associates' increases (raises), with the most money awarded to the number one spot, and then number two, and so on. The lowest-ranking person on the list may not be eligible for a raise; it just depends on his or her contributions. Gore feels strongly that this process does away with the unfairness of traditional systems in which one manager has complete control over subordinates' raises. Often, a manager is the only one who decides how much of a raise to give someone. What if your manager doesn't like you or is not aware of your true performance?

> *"Everybody here gets the same thing.*
> *There are no haves and have-nots."*

—Jeff Chambers, Vice President of Human Resources, SAS Institute

JetBlue follows what Mike Barger calls the "dude theory." "We're all dudes here—people with first names who get stuck in traffic, have to pay our taxes, and are tempted to bring more than 15 items into the grocery express line," Barger says. "It's a perspective that does a lot to connect people across our organization."

The word *employees* doesn't exist at JetBlue. In fact, it's used only once at JetBlue, during orientation, when the new hires are told, "We are not employees!" Everyone is considered a crew member, from customer-service crew members to technical operations and in-flight crew members.

JetBlue extends the fairness principle not only to its crew members but to its passengers, who are called "customers." All its aircraft feature roomy leather seats and an in-seat digital entertainment system with 36 channels of free DIRECTV programming.

Crews go to great lengths to make sure everyone is comfortable and well cared for.

Alston & Bird has made great strides in breaking down the class structure that is often inherent in law firms. "In our Atlanta office, we opened up what was once the attorney dining room to everyone in our organization," says Cathy Benton, chief human resources officer. Almost everyone said, "Well, it's about time!"

Con-way was established as a union-free environment to avoid what Pat Jannausch calls a "them-and-us mentality." This provides a more teamlike environment, Jannausch, says. "Our thinking was that people could move freely between and among the ranks, and an hourly employee could potentially be president of the company someday."

At Sallie Mae, hierarchy is avoided at all costs, according to Joni Reich, senior vice president of administration. "Our executives don't act like so-called executives," she says. "Everyone's on a first-name basis."

We're not suggesting that every status difference in your organization must be removed if you intend to enhance profits. When status differences can be justified for the value they add to the company, they're probably fine. However, providing thicker cushions for certain people does not fall into the category of value-added business practices. Look around your organization for status differences, for your bottles of Dasani. Are the status differences really needed, or can we all just have pitchers of water?

>> *What systems are in place to lead to the fairest workplace possible?*

Pathway #6: Build Trust into Your Culture

With high-profile corporate collapses and widespread damage to the public trust, we're in trust-challenged times. But never before has extending trust been so critical when discussing issues of workplace performance. In our consulting practice, clients continue to point to the erosion in trust, both in the workplace and in general. "We just don't feel as safe as we used to," a colleague says. "There doesn't seem to be anyone looking out for us anymore" was the sentiment offered in a recent focus group for managers at a local hospital.

When organizations feel the pressure to perform, they typically clamp down on people instead of extending trust. But trusting builds more trust, while not trusting results in more of what you already have.

Organizations that extend trust create environments in which what they do is what they say. They're places that give people the benefit of the doubt and where people always consider how what they do affects others. It's the job of leaders to extend trust first, paving the way for employees to extend trust to their colleagues and back to leaders.

SAS says it values trust and backs up its claim with action. "Trust for us is believing people will do the right thing for their customers and their work group," says HR Vice President Jeff Chambers.

When the company was deciding how to handle sick-time abuse, they replaced their sick-leave policy with a simple message to employees: Stay home if you're sick. Stay home with your kids if they're sick. Otherwise, we'll see you at work. No time allocations; no forms to fill out.

Imagine employees' surprise when they were presented with an honor system. SAS leadership was extending its trust. These days, SAS enjoys a decrease in the use of sick time. Are there still abusers? Very few. And those who take unfair advantage of the system meet a worse fate than a reprimand from their managers. They have to face their trustworthy teammates who had to take on extra work because of their absence. "Teammates are much more aggressive about confronting perceived abusers than managers ever were," says Chambers.

East Alabama Medical Center conducts random drug testing. If a person fails the test, he or she isn't automatically fired. Instead, the hospital extends its trust and assists that person in getting help. CEO Terry Andrus tells the story of a highly skilled nurse and father of three who was injured and then got hooked on painkillers. The hospital helped him get treatment, and, today, he's one of EAMC's most productive employees. "We'll do whatever it takes to help people with their problems rather than give up on them," says Andrus. "It's no different than what you'd do for a member of your family."

Omission of the Admission

How can you restore trust when you've lost it? Only one way works. Acknowledge that trust has been broken, explain why it happened, and state what you plan to do differently next time. Trust can be rebuilt, although it's more difficult to build it than to lose it.

At one of our workshops, a CEO acknowledged to his leadership team that trust had been broken. He emphasized his frustration by putting on the table a piece of rope that had been cut into two pieces. He stated that after trust has been broken, like the rope, it can never be as strong again.

This visual was certainly eye-opening, and all the team members, heads bowed, just stared at the rope. Luckily, the group included a former ropes course instructor. He leaped up, grabbed the two pieces of rope, and began tying them together in a knot that actually increased the rope's strength. He offered the thought that a rope, when broken and retied, can actually be stronger than it was originally. The instructor added that a knot-joined rope not only serves you better in the long run but is also a reminder of what we don't want to do again. The CEO smiled. It was a memorable event for the group and the CEO, who later admitted he had thought that rebuilding trust was impossible. He still has the rope in his office.

Every interaction between employees in your organization is an opportunity to either build or lose trust. For example, if the leadership team makes a decision that is bad for business but doesn't admit it, who's going to embrace their next decision? If a decision is bad, call it bad; openly acknowledge the mistake. Then, agree to put that decision behind you and move ahead. Otherwise, you can keep trying to extend trust, but people will never really believe you again.

> > *How do you extend trust in your organization? How do you rebuild it if it's broken?*

Pathway #7: Let Go of the Stagnant Quo

Most people are more comfortable with things as they are—what we call the "stagnant quo"—instead of what can be. It's an old joke that people who really want change, want to change back to the way it was!

What is the stagnant quo? It is the current system that isn't working, and everyone knows it, yet it's still "how we do business." It may be a trap you've gotten into by just telling people what they want to hear because that's much easier than sharing with them what's really going on. It might also be doing what you've always done because no one will notice if you do things differently, giving only what you have to give because if you try to do more and fail, you'll risk looking incompetent.

>> *What parts of your organization are stuck in the stagnant quo? Why have these issues remained unresolved for so long?*

We keep things as they are out of fear—fear of delving into the unknown, of looking bad, of being embarrassed, of not fitting in. Efforts to avoid these things add up, day by day, so we're maintaining the stagnant quo instead of taking risks that could propel ourselves and the organization forward.

How does the quo become stagnant? Traditionally, it's handed down from one employee to another, one interaction at a time, and is kept neatly in place. It's reinforced in your organization by what gets attention, what is rewarded, and what is punished.

JetBlue bucked the stagnant quo with its launch in 2000. No one believed the company could run a profitable airline out of New York. But JetBlue saw things differently. The company believed New York was a prime choice for its business base, with 20 million people living in the boroughs of Manhattan, many of whom liked to travel, and New York the number one travel destination in the United States. The company has defied its critics by becoming one of the fastest-growing airlines in the world, top-ranked two years in a row in the industry's Airline Quality Rating study.

Bright Grey, a life insurance company established in Edinburgh, Scotland, in 2001, positions itself as a "life protection" brand. As a relatively new operation, Bright Grey made the decision to color outside the lines of its industry's traditional approach by not following the stagnant quo and by redefining standards. Its Destination was to challenge conventional practices within the protection market. According to CEO David Robinson, the company determined it would challenge outdated practices and build stronger, trusting relationships with customers so as to provide a genuine hand up as opposed to a handout.

The name *Bright Grey* reflects the contrast the company offers in a market perceived to be gray, complex, and confusing. A pink dot over the *i* in *Bright* represents the bright spot in a gray world.

What makes Bright Grey different is its customer-first philosophy, demonstrated through simplicity, clarity, and a common-sense approach in serving customers. It hires people with a can-do attitude and a passion for service. We witnessed this first-hand when we participated in the 15-minute morning gathering, where a team member led the daily round-circle discussion focused on one of the core principles. In the morning line-up, participants gave updates on the business and explored additional ways of delivering on the brand promise. They also acknowledged special events, birthdays, and anniversaries. On that same day, the CEO had his weekly 30-minute update and Q&A session with the entire staff.

The future looks bright for this innovative company. Staff doubled in the first year. Revenues doubled in 2004 and are still growing, more proof that People = Profits.

> **>> How are you encouraging people to let go of the stagnant quo?**

Stagnant quos are ripe for finding and challenging. Ask about those things that don't make sense to you and about the history behind a policy, plan, or practice. The minute you hear anyone say, "That's just how we've always done it," you've probably found the stagnant quo. We encourage you to go after it! Your ability to inquire about a history, rationale, or understanding is most powerful inside an organization. We like the question that begins "Help me understand this. . . ." It may just open up the dialogue to a whole new way of doing business, and, at a minimum, it certainly brings some badly needed attention to the issues everyone talks about, whether in conference rooms, hallways, or around the watercooler!

Pathways to Profitability

1. Get the right destination

2. Connect people to the business

3. Know who you really are

4. Cultivate commitment, not compliance

5. Create an equitable experience for your people

6. Build trust into your culture

7. Let go of the stagnant quo

[3] THE 4-A PROCESS

A Tool for Maximizing
Business Growth

Often, the only constant we have in business today is change. From emerging technologies to encroaching competitors, binding government regulations to Wall Street expectations, change bombards us from every direction, bringing with it the need for adaptation—at lightning speed. There is not a business in existence today that would not benefit from reinventing itself. As the business environment continues its rapid transformation, businesses that go on as they always have will undoubtedly perform with less success in the future. In every organization of every size, leaders must learn to rally their organizations, galvanizing people to adapt swiftly and effectively to conditions that will help them be more competitive. How you respond to these external forces sets the course for whether your business will soar, shrink, become irrelevant, or perhaps even cease to exist.

No organization is impervious to tough times. Yet, as success guru Napoleon Hill says, "every negative event contains within it the seed of an equal or greater benefit." Keeping the focus on the seeds hidden in what might appear to be negative events, we pose these questions:

- In the midst of these challenging times, what is the equal or greater benefit for your organization?

- What enables you to compete successfully?

- Is it your leadership, your people, your purpose, or your customers who may be demanding more attention than ever before?

When considering these questions with our clients, we've found that some or all of the seeds for success are already planted in every organization. They can be brought to fruition by a single organizational competency: the organization's ability to adapt, to move from inertia to innovation, control to growth, busyness to business contribution, misalignment to focus, and stagnation to adaptation.

Reaction to Change

You've heard before that it's not what happens to you that matters but how you react to it. We think this timeless adage is true, yet it also leaves a lot to fate in the unforgiving world of business. Of the 12 largest companies that existed in 1900, only 1—General Electric—is still around today. The other leading companies were outpaced and have gone out of business or been scooped up into someone else's ideas. We think that instead of waiting around for change to find you, your organization should be the change the world needs and should look for every opportunity to get ready. That way, you're not trying to change with the added pressures of "having to" but can adapt beforehand or create the change, all on your own terms.

>> *How ready for change is the average person*
in your organization?

Although no organization should believe it can control change, it's important to understand how to maximize performance while going through it, which is basically every day! Any organization that's forced to change or has change imposed on it cannot hope to compete with organizations that understand the signals of change and adapt ahead of time. Bill McGowan, who founded MCI in the late 1960s, shares his insights on change: "The only practice that's constant now is the practice of constantly accommodating to change—and if you're not changing constantly, you're probably not going to be accommodating the reality of your world."[1]

Kmart has been forced to adapt, not necessarily because it wanted to, but because consumers compelled its adaptation by choosing to spend more hard-earned dollars at Kmart's prime competitors, Wal-Mart and Target. (We explore these three seemingly similar but vastly different companies in chapter 7.)

In many ways, then, change has been around longer than any organization and perhaps has been the variable most woven through the history of business. We still have much to learn about change because it's a difficult process to live through, talk about, and certainly write about, yet it's in our best interests to learn as much about change as change has to teach us.

Put yourself for a moment in the role of an external consultant and consider the following questions:

- What do you see happening inside your organization that seems out of alignment with the outside world?

- What do your customers crave that you can't provide today? In other words, what are your customers willing to give you more cash for that you're not supplying to them today?

- What will they be buying over the next two years, and what will the next generation of customers need from your organization? And, even more important, will you be ready to give it to them?

We will help you explore these crucial questions, which provide topics we hope will dominate your internal meeting agendas and spark exceptional debates about your organization's future.

> >> *How adaptable is your organization to the events around you?*

Is change easy? Of course not. It's painfully difficult sometimes. Most of us are better at doing what we've always done than trying new ways of accomplishing our aims. Ironically, the success that many businesses have had over the past 10 years has led to a complacency that may hold them hostage to their histories.

Doing Change Right

A lot of the pain of change could be surmounted by doing change right—being up front with employees and involving them in business realities. Involvement is particularly critical when downsizing.

Sallie Mae has gone out of its way to make separation as painless as possible for its employees. As the company grew, acquiring more than a dozen companies since 1997, redundant operations and staff positions resulted, causing some employees to lose their jobs.

"Whenever we need to separate individuals through no fault of their own, we go out of our way to really support them . . . in their transition to new employment."

—Joni Reich, Vice President of Administration, Sallie Mae

"As we've acquired companies, we've had to streamline," says Reich. "That's always painful, but it's part of business. We really take it to heart. I think that's one of our hallmarks. Our employees know that we'll always be straightforward with them in sharing information about our business and what we need to do to be successful." It goes a long way, Reich says, not only in making sure the employee leaves the company in the best way possible but also in reassuring the workforce that they will always be treated fairly and respectfully—even if a position is eliminated or a work site closed because of an acquisition.

Sallie Mae offers training assistance, sets up career centers on-site, and reaches out to employees in every way to help them land on their feet. The company has even offered "money-back guarantees" to employers who hire displaced Sallie Mae workers. If the employee is terminated for poor attendance or performance in the first six months, the hiring company can be paid as much as $10,000.

Corning Incorporated, too, faced a drastic layoff with the solid resolve to do the right thing by its employees. In 2001, the company was forced to cut its 40,000-person workforce in half, when "the bottom fell out" of the telecommunications industry, its major customer. Telecom companies, many of which went bankrupt, stopped buying Corning's bread-and-butter product, optical fiber. Gail Baity, vice president of human resources, says, "Although it was a traumatic experience for all of us, we devoted ourselves to treating people with the utmost care in making their transition."

Corning provided financial and job support and created a special panel tasked with ensuring that all planned staffing reductions were well thought out. The company also converted its 90-person recruiting organization into an outplacement support group. "Our assumption was, they knew the industries to look for in bringing our people to Corning and would know the industries to help them relocate," Baity explains. At the same time, Corning's "Talent to Talent" initiative kept track of all former employees so they could be easily located in the future. "Not only did we want our people to land on solid ground on their way out; we wanted to make sure that if business turned around again, they would want to return to us—and many have."

Same Ol' Same Ol'

Whenever you see signs of your organization trying to do the "same ol' same ol'," remind everyone of the history of the U.S. auto industry. General Motors at one time claimed 60 percent of the U.S. auto market. Today, all U.S. automakers sell less than 60 percent combined. Complacency is an expensive and dreadful approach. The Big Three automakers in the United States—Ford, GM, and Chrysler (now DaimlerChrysler)—have each worked to stay competitive but have tried to perform in a new market planked by the need for speed, service, and innovation, all qualities they would like to be known for but aren't.

While speed, service, and innovation are traits within each company's grasp, the Big Three are in many ways prisoners of their pasts. Years of strained relationships with workforces have led to a cycle of mistrust, gas prices are soaring, effective new ways of curtailing the money drain elude them, and, all the while, overseas competitors continue their domination.

Certainly, part of the growth of automakers outside the United States has been the result of expanding into new markets and reaching new buyers. Before announcing its decision to permanently shut down Oldsmobile, GM launched the "It's not your father's Oldsmobile" campaign to lure a new generation of buyers. The problem was that the younger generation of buyers didn't think of their dads' Oldsmobiles; they thought of their grandfathers' Oldsmobiles! Most younger car buyers simply had much hipper options. Before wading into battle, then, the tactics, strategies, and products of today's consumer must be understood with absolute certainty. Without this understanding, businesses will continuously fall short of everyone's expectations.

> > *Can you change the direction of your organization quickly in order to stay competitive?*

Not the Easy Way Out

It's tempting for organizations to look for quick fixes to their problems—any strategy to avoid changing how they work. But taking the easy way out doesn't work. We've found that most such shortcuts only lead to places that are worse than where you started. Being able to adapt to new situations requires constant attention to details, strategies, interactions, and, of course, people. Certainly a lot to manage while you're trying to make money, too!

Have you ever thought about why people typically resist change? Is it simply fear of the unknown? Or maybe fear of the known? We think it comes down to the basic human desire to be comfortable and competent. And when we are faced with the threat of becoming uncomfortable or incompetent, as always happens with change, we withdraw in hopes that we may avoid having to live uncomfortably, or being perceived as incompetent, or both.

> >> *Do your people see changes that could benefit your business but they aren't speaking up?*

Consider that, right now, as your organization plans to do what it has always done, another organization is preparing to move in on your customers. How will you stop that company? What do you have in your organization that will enable you to keep your current primary customers and attract new ones? In our research, we've found that the companies that adapt best to change are those that have firmly defined their Destinations, focused their workforces, and continuously look ahead to what's coming—not back at what's happened. Anybody can look back. The defining skill is being able to look ahead and make calculated decisions for your business and for your people.

> *"There's a lot of baggage—pun intended—with new hires who come from our industry. We eagerly share our commitment to help change their experience."*
>
> —Captain Mike Barger, Vice President and
> Chief Learning Officer, JetBlue Airways

We don't want you to ignore the past. Just the opposite. We want you to use it as one predictor of the future—learn from it but don't rely on it. We do, however, want you to see the current reality and understand it so well that you are able to determine a course of events and interactions that leads your business to perform. It's important to know that any future state of your organization cannot be understood by looking at your past; it must be made by looking at what you have today and knowing what you want to achieve tomorrow.

We don't have a business crystal ball, so how do we see into the future? We must learn to see what's happening today and blend that with where we want to be tomorrow. This is, in short, the essence of business—the ability to survive through adaptation. Given the clear and relentless pursuit of survival and growth, organizations that take too long to make things happen are simply left behind. We argue here that it's better to make slight adjustments continuously than to implement periodic large-scale changes in reaction to external, often debilitating, influences. Every organization can respond to change, but not every organization responds before change is imposed.

> > *What signs alert you to the need for change? What have you missed in the past three years that should have been a signal for change?*

SAS Institute: A Case in Point

In 2002, in a downturn economy, SAS Institute pulled off an excellent example of adaptation, leaving the company miles ahead of others in its industry with its greatest source of competitive advantage, its people. SAS leadership decided to forgo profitability and hire more aggressively than ever before. While most companies were expanding at the rate of 1 percent in 2002, SAS increased its U.S. workforce by a whopping 7 percent. Consider the implications of this highly calculated strategy. As other companies, including SAS's competitors, worried about the economy, SAS adapted by having a hiring fest.

"We hired 600 people from a variety of backgrounds, from financial services to retail to manufacturing," says Jeff Chambers, vice president of human resources at SAS. "Many of them had experienced 'economic dislocation' with our competitors. We believed that when the economy improved, these new hires would be committed SAS employees. Our decision hurt short-term profitability, but it was a good long-term strategy. When things turned around, we were well positioned to dominate."

> *"Management's philosophy is always to ask 'How are you doing?' as opposed to 'What are you doing?'"*
> —Jeff Chambers, Vice President of Human Resources, SAS Institute

Because it had enough cash, SAS could respond far better than its competitors did when hard times hit the technology sector. However, other firms with just as much cash didn't act. So what enabled SAS to do something that kept it ahead of the change? The company was acutely aware of its defined goals, aligned itself organizationally to achieve them, held itself accountable for achieving them, and then adapted by making tweaks. By communicating its hiring strategy to employees and preparing them for a 10 percent decrease in profit share, SAS kept its people on board with the ultimate Destination: helping them adapt to temporary discomfort through the promise of long-term gain. It was a bold and remarkable move, and it's exactly what business today is all about.

The 4-A Process

What do companies like SAS know that others don't? We talked with leaders from SAS and several other forward-looking organizations in order to capture their strategic thinking, planning, and execution processes. This is what we found: When organizations can adapt, they follow a similar set of steps.

The more we looked at these companies, the more revealing those steps became. In fact, we found that achieving the best results in building a forward-thinking, adaptable organization— one that transcends the stagnant quo—had little to do with the traditionally espoused models of change. It had to do with people being intricately connected to the business and moving the business forward in an adaptive way.

The result is our 4-A Process, a tool for maximizing business growth, shown in Figure 2. It divides the thinking process into four continuous phases: Awareness, Alignment, Accountability, and Adaptation. Each step is followed by action.

Together, the 4-As provide a unique route to improved performance. Some of your organization's everyday activities may already fit into one of these categories. The 4-A Process organizes activities into a continuous flow that helps your organization focus its thinking, assess progress, identify gaps, and make small adjustments to stay on course. It serves as a guide for answering four key questions at the individual, team, and organizational levels:

1. **Awareness:** What is your Destination or Destinations?

2. **Alignment:** What do you need to do to focus on achieving the Destination? How do you align the organization so that you are all working toward the Destination?

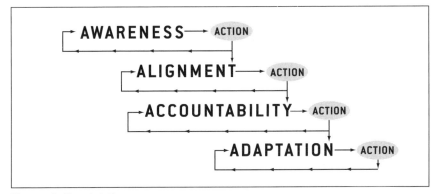

Figure 2. The 4-A Process

3. **Accountability:** How are Destination-supporting behaviors reinforced?

4. **Adaptation:** How do you make slight adjustments that will keep you winning, continuously, in any kind of circumstance?

The 4-As can be used to help an organization adapt to change, or, in our parlance, reach any Destination. The ultimate Destination or goal of the 4-A Process is to help people and organizations learn faster than the world around them is changing. As a result, they stay fresh, agile, and quicker than their competition in reaching their Destinations. (Chapters 4 through 7 explore each step in depth.)

Three Levels of Effectiveness

The 4-A Process is designed to work on three levels: organizational, team, and individual. You can put it in place at all levels, regardless of your business, the size of your company, the industry you work in, or your organization's history. When leadership decides to set an organizational Destination, the team and individual Destinations must align and create a unified focus for the organization. It's true that an organization will have multiple Destinations, as will teams and individuals. However, each organization's overarching Desti-nation is the guiding force for behaviors at all levels and without exceptions.

While we don't suggest that hovering over people is any way to get things done, we do suggest having little tolerance for any behavior or activity that deviates from the agreed-on and well-understood organizational Destination. In a healthy organization, this approach will be welcomed. In an unhealthy one, it will be seen as complete anarchy. If an organization's culture and focus have not emphasized high performance and output, it's critical that teams and individuals be prepared for new standards before formally adopting Destinations as a focus tool. Let your workforce know that you are indeed making a shift, why you are making it, what the new way of doing business will look like, and what the advantages will be to the organization, teams, individuals, and customers. In fact, having a change-ready organization is a great Destination—and could very likely be one of your first as you work through the 4-A Process! Let's look further at each level.

Organization

We can use the 4-As to trace the remarkable organizational success of Southwest Airlines. Since 1971, Southwest has pursued its Destination of "The 3 LFs": Low Fares, Lots of Flights, and Lots of Fun. In the Awareness step, the company created a mission statement and values that supported its identity as an organization, and, most important, it defined where it wanted to go—what service it could offer that other airlines did not. In the Alignment step, Southwest hired people who could deliver directly on the Destination. In Accountability, leaders helped people understand the critical importance of their role in reaching the Destination and then held them accountable for their contributions by creating a first-class culture in a discount airline. With these steps firmly in place, Southwest was ready for the fourth step, Adaptation—the ability to anticipate and adapt to external conditions. With its industry radar always on, the company could keep a constant eye on what was up ahead and adjust its organizational flight plan as needed.

Southwest Airlines developed a gift for delivering a superior product for a low price. The company also learned how to compete on virtually every aspect of business, including marketing, sales, and its now-legendary customer and employee loyalty. Having started as an underdog against the giants of the time, Braniff and Texas Internataional, Southwest leaders leveraged their start-up status to create a "crusade" against the big guys. Their tenacity and spirit paid off in profits!

The airline's ability to stay ahead of the competition paid off again in November 2001. When oil prices started to climb, the company prepurchased enough fuel to last through the next nine years. Since then, Southwest's aggressive hedging program has shielded it from soaring oil prices, delivering profits while its rivals have posted billions of dollars in losses. Southwest Executive Chairman Herb Kelleher is always on the lookout for anything that might get in the way of his airline's ability to be profitable. He once joked that he was accused of predicting 11 of the past 3 recessions!

Team

The 4-A Process applies to any team Destination and should be aligned with organizational Destinations. However, because of team dynamics and individual personalities, teams often need to establish other Destinations for themselves, usually centered on performance.

Let's take, for example, building a high-performance team. In Awareness, you paint a picture of where you want to be compared to where you are today and, at the same time, you establish the metrics or signals that will tell you when you've arrived. In Alignment, you set people up to succeed, reinforcing and rewarding behavior that's aligned with the Destination. In Accountability, you apply healthy pressure to keep performance high and continue to reward behaviors needed to achieve the Destination. In Adaptation, when the team has reached a level of optimum performance, you teach team members to make slight adjustments based on changing needs, such as when new people join the team, a new competitor enters your market space, or another department changes its practices and affects your ability to get things done.

To help gear up for applying the 4-As to your organization or team, answer the questions in Exercise 2, on page 104, as a group.

Individual

The 4-As help individuals set, focus, and reach their professional and personal goals, from charting a career path to improving specific areas of performance. At work, it's important to allow Destinations to be both personal and professional, ensuring, of course, that professional Destinations ultimately help the business perform or gravitate toward organizational Destinations.

For example, if one of your Destinations is to be a better public speaker, you can set that as your personal Destination and create the most direct, least resistant path to getting there. Thus, in Awareness, set your Destination of effective public speaking, or you might break that into smaller Destinations such as giving a five-minute speech to your family, then your best friend, your team, and so on. Closely examine your capabilities when you speak in front of groups. Then, in Alignment, put yourself in situations in which your public-speaking skills can effectively and efficiently develop. In Accountability, ensure that you are practicing, eliciting feedback, improving, and moving toward your ultimate Destination. In Adaptation, after you've reached your Destination of being a better speaker, find new ways of refining your presentations and achieving even better results. Eventually, you may even begin coaching others. Remember, the biggest hurdle will be to reach the threshold of being able to adapt to new situations with ease and finesse. All along, you'll be enhancing your capabilities for effective public speaking.

Use the questions in Exercise 3, on page 105, to guide your 4-A Process.

Exercise (2)	
APPLYING THE 4-A PROCESS TO ORGANIZATIONS AND TEAMS	
4-As for Reaching Our Destination	**Preparing for the Outcome**
Awareness How will we determine our Destination?	How will we know that everyone understands and supports the Destination?
Alignment What will we need to do to get everything focused on reaching the Destination?	How will we know that people, processes, and systems are aligned to reach the Destination?
Accountability What behaviors will demonstrate our support of the Destination? How will these be communicated and measured?	How will we demonstrate personal accountability and commitment? Once we reach the Destination, how will we celebrate?
Adaptation How will we make ongoing adjustments?	What systems will be in place for determining when adjustments need to be made and when they're successful?

Division of Labor = Division of Focus

Many organizations rely on past business models that no longer yield the same results in today's business environment as they

Exercise (3)	
APPLYING THE 4-A PROCESS TO INDIVIDUALS	
4-As for Reaching My Individual Destination	**Preparing for the Outcome**
Awareness How will I decide on a Destination?	Who will support me in reaching my Destination?
Alignment What will I need to do to focus everything on reaching my Destination?	How will I know that all the resources I need to reach my Destination are aligned?
Accountability What behaviors will demonstrate my support of my Destination? How will these be communicated and measured?	How will I hold myself accountable? Once I reach my Destination, how will I celebrate?
Adaptation How will I make ongoing adjustments?	How will I know if and when future adjustments need to be made?

did previously. Most highly successful companies were formed from a division-of-labor model based on numerous parts—departments—that do their own thing and eventually produce a product or service. For a long time, this model worked. But, today, it's a different environment, and the division-of-labor model has resulted in a division-of-focus approach.

Passengers on a fully booked flight boarded a plane and then sat for several hours at the gate in an airport in Phoenix, Arizona. The aircraft couldn't take off because the supervising mechanic refused to send for the on-call mechanic. It turned out that the closest mechanic had already worked 40 hours that week, and the supervising mechanic was instructed to limit overtime no matter what the circumstances.

As the hours passed, so did the fliers' patience. A mechanic was finally dispatched nearly five hours later, once the supervisor got a call from the VP overseeing maintenance. The original cost to the airline for overtime would have been $160, but instead, the cost of the ripple effect of other flights delayed, lost revenue, lost customers, frustrated employees, and on and on, was several thousand dollars.

An organization is only as strong as its weakest point of contact with a customer. In this case, the airline lost on every possible interaction, including the supervising mechanic, who followed orders and ended up being reprimanded for the loss of revenue and complaints received from this flight. Had this airline been on board with the 4-A Process, there probably would have been a different outcome—one in which behaviors were totally focused on the customer experience rather than on departmental edicts, managed in isolation.

Big Changes Sometimes, Small Changes All the Time

The 4-A Process uses a perspective that differs from those of traditional change models. Traditional models are built on the premise that organizations change when the pain of their current way of doing things becomes more painful than the pain of changing. We call this a total waste of time, resources, and opportunity! What typically happens is that everyone, including your customers, goes through a lot of needless agony.

The 4-A Process looks at change prospectively. It encourages and guides leaders of organizations to look for opportunities to make slight adjustments rather than large-scale changes that are often difficult to manage and sustain. Note that you'll sometimes need large-scale change initiatives to build momentum inside your organization and reach your intended levels of performance. Large-scale changes, however, are costly and time consuming. Use them only when absolutely necessary, such as when you need to completely redirect your culture or business model or adjust to a major initiative such as a merger, an acquisition, or a threat from a new competitor. Although you'll have to face external forces regardless of readiness, the goal is to be so well prepared that you can easily adapt to changes and stay ahead of your competition.

Say that one of your Destinations is to be a great workplace. You make large-scale changes, to the point that you reach a key threshold: perhaps 85 percent of your people confirm that it's a great workplace. At that point, in the Adaptation phase, you make small adjustments to sustain your Destination through any internal fluctuation or external threat. Teaching your organization to recognize the need and have the ability to adapt is critical and will be a skill you can use continuously.

Have you ever seen the reality show *The Amazing Race*? What is the common competence of the winning teams? It's that they adapt to any situation, any new challenge, and do so without a lot of disruption to their ability to execute. We want you to be an amazing company, to compete with vigor and resolve regardless of what your competition or other external threats put in front of you.

The individual steps of the 4-A Process—Awareness, Alignment, Accountability, and Adaptation—will look different from one organization to the next, depending on the organization's life cycle, size, and current state of operations and the nature of its business. If you're a start-up, chances are that you can move through the first three steps quickly because flexibility is greatest in the early stages of an organization's life cycle. If you're a large and long-established organization, though, you may need a time-consuming overhaul, depending on the modification you're trying to make. The goal is to move as many issues as possible through the first three steps and into the fourth step, Adaptation. This means you will be able to constantly adapt in small ways rather than make huge changes that are often more costly in time, energy, and resources. Large-scale change generally gets a bad rap from employees because it leads to confusion and causes people to disengage. Even the best-managed large-scale change creates more chaos in the front end and, over time, levels out to less confusion. Eventually, you land at your Destination.

The sequence in this model is always the same—Awareness, Alignment, Accountability, and Adaptation—although the duration of each step depends on variables such as the organization's current state, its closeness to the Destination, the size of its workforce, and its current workload. These factors influence its ability to focus on reaching the Destination. If you go out of sequence, such as trying to align people without first making them aware of what they're aligning to, it simply doesn't work. If you try to hold people accountable for what they should be doing, regardless of whether they understand how what they do aligns with the goal, you move into a relationship of compliance rather than of commitment. You should intentionally avoid this dynamic in any step of the 4-A Process.

Major Surgery Prevention

If we look at an organization as a living system, like the human body, we see a thriving "being" whose health creates forward momentum. When it's kept in good shape, major surgery isn't needed.

Unfortunately, most change initiatives and theories are based on a "wait until you're very sick" methodology, which doesn't make a lot of sense! The 4-A Process makes your Destination a healthy one so that you never have to go under the knife. None of us wants the pain and expense of major surgery. It's invasive, it causes downtime, and it doesn't always cure. Not to mention the fact that it is really scary!

Changing habits and staying healthy aren't easy. A study published in *Fast Company*, "Change or Die," found that, even after major bypass surgery, 9 out of 10 patients reverted to their bad lifestyle habits.[2] If death isn't a compelling enough reason to change, it's not surprising that we don't pay attention to symptoms warning us of disease. We don't know how many of these patients might have benefited from using our 4-A Process. But we do hope that your use of this thinking process results in change for everyone, including those whose bad habits have an adverse effect on themselves, their teams and customers, and the organizations in which they work.

When considering change, remember that the best time to make it happen is before it's needed. It's like learning to climb a mountain. The worst time to learn how to climb one is when you're standing in front of it. Trying to change when you're faced with the critical need to do so is daunting—and often leads to unnecessary stress, even chaos, for the organization and its people.

> **>> *Is your organization a candidate for major surgery, or for minor tweaks?***

Today's business environment leaves little room for learning, especially when the demands of competing change so quickly and customers' needs are so immediate. The 4-A Process helps you avoid major surgery in your organization by getting healthy in Awareness, Alignment, and Accountability and then continuing to make slight adjustments in Adaptation.

[4] AWARENESS

Planning Your Destination

Great leaders are like pilots. They know exactly where they're going and how long it will take to get there, see the path ahead, make adjustments during the trip so as to avoid unpleasant and unnecessary delays, and stay on course to reach their Destinations safely. The really great ones call out points of interest and, most of all, help everybody enjoy the flight. Meanwhile, passengers—employees, customers, and other stakeholders—trust their pilot to get them to the right Destination, to keep them informed along the way, especially if changes in direction are needed, and to do everything possible to ensure a successful journey.

The first step of the 4-A Process, Awareness, helps leaders be better organizational pilots. It's a tool for determining where your organization is going, bringing people on board, and navigating intentionally toward each Destination. We call this *Destination Planning.*

An organization's Destinations are designed to help achieve the organization's overall mission. While an organization has only one mission or vision, it may have multiple Destinations and may add new ones in response to changes in the marketplace. Destinations most resemble goals, yet we have intentionally focused on the word *Destination* because a goal doesn't automatically imply focused execution and a Destination includes built-in action. A Destination activates the whole organization, as it implies that this is a place everyone must strive to reach. We view a goal as something to simply achieve, but a Destination is something that has meaning throughout the organization and provides the focus needed to work toward achieving it.

If a business is to flourish, every person in the organization must be able to answer three fundamental questions:

1. Where is our organization going?
2. What competencies are we using to get there?
3. How does our organization ultimately make money?

If you don't know the answers for your organization, please put down this book now and find out what they are! If you ask and others don't know, pull everyone together and work it out on the spot. For each day these three questions go unanswered, your competition becomes stronger and you give away an opportunity to progress toward profitability.

Destination Planning helps you focus on where your organization is going and grow the competencies you will use to get there. It will also increase your organization's profits. It's a crucial skill for leaders and employees. If used at every level of the organization, the chances of everyone reaching the same Destination together are much greater.

The Focus

The fundamental outcome of Awareness is *focus*—a condition in which something can be clearly perceived. Think about a time when you were at the movie theater and the picture on the screen was blurry. Most likely, the audience began to grumble, people turned around and glared at the projection booth and, eventually, someone yelled "Focus!" There was frustration because no one could see what was happening. Some people thought about leaving. Finally, the projectionist adjusted the focus, the picture became clear, and the audience cheered. In the same way, a good leader needs to refine focus for the organization and make sure that everyone can see with clarity.

As we've mentioned, the goal of any business is to stay in business. The strength of an organization is its ability to manage and accelerate profitable growth. This happens best when the entire organization is focused and delivering on its promise to internal and external stakeholders. Yet, organizations often lose their focus or never really have one to begin with. Does anyone understand why Sears went into the auto insurance business? Or why Kmart bought Borders?

Focus helps you stay relevant—relevant to your customers, board, employees, and community. It's incredibly painful to be in an organization that's on its way to irrelevance. Without a common focus, everyone may be moving, but in different directions.

> >> *Where does your organization get its focus? Are you actively piloting it to its Destination, or are you on automatic pilot, just going along for the ride?*

Organizations become irrelevant by losing sight of what they do best, by not keeping skills sharp at the team and individual levels, and by not understanding what's going on in the competitive world around them. Even when the workforce is on board, an irrelevant Destination, one without purpose and meaning, can land you in a place to which you did not intend to travel. Destination Planning is an effective and purposeful way of protecting against irrelevance.

Destinations, however, can be difficult to pin down. They ask you to commit to where you're going and to bring everybody along. It's easier to stay vague, but that's a costly decision. Staying vague may involve less attachment and less fear of choosing the wrong path, yet it also could mean less success if you do manage to reach a profitable Destination. Vague Destinations are breeding grounds for antiquated behaviors and old-school thinking, since it really doesn't matter what you do when you don't know where you're going. Plus, if you don't know where you're going, how do you ever know that you got anywhere?

Over the centuries, sailors have used different methods of navigation. The earliest seafarers kept in sight of land, sailing along the coast from landmark to landmark until they reached their Destination. This was not always the most direct route. Eventually, sailors began to look to the sky. By keeping the North Star always in sight, they freed themselves from the coast and could reach their Destination more quickly. All the people on the boat understood this and could easily see the course that lay before them. When your Destination is constantly in sight, it can truly drive your business toward the highest returns on your investments.

> *>> How relevant is your organization today? Is any part of your organization becoming less relevant? What needs to change if you are going to stay competitive?*

An Extraordinary Destination

As we begin to explore Awareness, let's look first at an organization whose Destination profoundly affects the lives of every U.S. inhabitant, every hour of every day: U.S. Customs and Border Protection (CBP).

When President George W. Bush established the U.S. Department of Homeland Security, he consolidated parts of the U.S. Customs Service, the Immigration and Naturalization Service (INS), and the Animal and Plant Inspection Service, along with 11,000 Border Patrol agents, into the CBP. Through this new organization, the president redefined the nation's counterterrorism role with the One Face at the Border program as its Destination.

Commissioner Robert C. Bonner and his leadership team created a clear priority mission for their new agency of 42,000 people, which included 30,000 CBP officers, CBP agriculture specialists, and CBP Border Patrol agents. The priority mission of protecting the country is one to which every person can connect, tactically, operationally, and emotionally. Bonner also clearly defined the end state or Destination: one agency of the U.S. government to manage and control the nation's borders.

> *"Our Destination is an extraordinary one: Protecting*
> *our country and preventing terrorists or terrorist*
> *weapons from getting into the United States."*
>
> —Robert C. Bonner, Commissioner,
> U.S. Customs and Border Protection

Imagine taking these four agencies and melding them into one unified, high-performing agency with the critical task of shielding the United States from terrorist threats. Unification was complicated because each agency did things differently. "We had four different salary or grade structures, four different overtime systems, four different uniforms, four different badges, different weapons, different training policies, and different bargaining units," Commissioner Bonner explains. To build consensus and offer guidance on the many issues involved in unification, he launched the Transition Management Office, bringing together the best thinkers from the four merging agencies.

Agents were cross-trained and given the same uniforms at all points of entry—one badge and patch designating all of our law enforcement personnel as CBP. The shared vision of One Face at the Border was continuously communicated and reinforced so that everyone could understand and take pride in the ultimate mission of protecting the United States against terrorism. "Change is always difficult for people," Commissioner Bonner observes. "But if people understand what the change is, why it's taking place, and where you're going, they will accept it far faster."

> > *CBP created a new, unified vision as a result of a major crisis. In your organization, do you create your Destination because there's a crisis or because there's an opportunity?*

Cabin Preparation for Take-Off

It makes a pilot's job much easier when the passengers all know where the plane is going—and all of them actually want to go there! Imagine if you had a plane headed to Detroit that was full of passengers who wanted to go to Las Vegas, or perhaps to 15 different places! Crew members would suddenly have much more to do than serve drinks and peanuts; they would be trying to sell grumpy passengers on the benefits of Detroit.

In fact, have you ever been on a flight that had to divert to another city because of some unforeseen circumstance? Once the passengers are told that they must go someplace else, you'll typically hear a lot of sighs and grumbles. Free drinks start rolling out to make amends, all because the destination is different than planned. We believe organizations that are not clear about their Destinations spend an enormous amount of time serving free drinks—in other words, trying to appease workers. That's because although changing directions is problematic, not having one to begin with is even worse!

No leader intends his or her organization to be unclear about its Destination. In fact, as a leader, you're probably extremely clear about where your organization is going and have made it clear to every person who's on board. But, if you know where your organization is going, and you've told everyone in the organization many times where you're going, why, then, six months later, is your organization still on the ground? Maybe employees didn't have the tools they needed to begin, let alone complete, the journey. Or maybe the passengers all agreed with your flight plan, but just before the cabin door was about to shut and the plane was ready to take off, the counter-talk of "that'll never work here" began.

Are naysayers bad people? No, and as frustrating as this behavior is, we should expect people to resist when they're not truly on board with your Destination. The number one reason employees do not get on board is that they simply don't understand their role in making the Destination happen. If your employees don't see both the Destination and how their jobs help the organization get there, you won't have the clarity you need to make them major contributors.

>> *If you've set your Destination, are your people all
on board? Do your people understand their roles
in making the Destination happen?*

Channels of Input

The best way to get people on board with your Destination is to
invite them to chart it with you. Most of the information you
need to compete thoughtfully and win is inside your organization. Open up all channels of input so that ideas flow quickly
from your entire organization. To ensure that your organization
is on track in soliciting feedback from your stakeholders and
implementing Destinations, we recommend appointing a *Destination Champion,* or *DC,* for your organization and also one for
each team. (We'll explore the role of the DC in chapter 5.)

Some leaders assume the lower ranks have no strategic insight
to offer. This can be an incredibly expensive point of view. Sony's
PlayStation was first suggested by a mid-level employee, who was
quickly told by senior leadership that Sony was not in the game
business. He didn't listen to them and found ways to make
PlayStation a Destination. Good thing. PlayStation now accounts
for 60 percent of Sony's profits!

>> *In setting your Destination, how are you soliciting feed-
back from your different stakeholders? How are you
weighing the relative importance of each stakeholder
group in reaching your Destination?*

After gathering input, synthesize it and chart your course.
State the Destination as clearly as possible, in one simple, specific
sentence. For example, "In every market we're in, we will have
the number-one- or number-two-selling product." Destinations

must always be articulated so that people can live them. Traditional vision statements have often failed to deliver on their intended purpose because they're too lofty, or vague, or removed from everyday reality. If your Destination is more than a sentence long, you run the risk that people won't get it. And they need to get it!

Make it believable. People are already inundated with too much corporate jargon. The minute words like reengineering, restructuring, and rightsizing come out, people begin thinking of, and yearning for, simpler days. Next thing you know, heads are nodding, but not in agreement with your Destination.

One of our favorite Destination stories—a lesson in simplicity, if ever there was one—happened years ago, when an executive from Oracle was discussing his strategy for moving forward. He didn't call it a Destination, yet we thought it was one of pure brilliance. When pressed for the single most important goal for Oracle, he scribbled something down on a small piece of paper and ran to put it on the overhead projector. It read simply, "Kill Microsoft." The audience went nuts, and it was a terrific start to galvanizing the workforce toward a collective Destination. Imagine, two words, put together in the right context, drove an organization into action.

Along with focusing on the big-picture Destination, break your journey down into smaller, closer, short-term Destinations. See what's needed on the immediate horizon.

At SAS Institute, Jeff Chambers, VP of human resources, sums up SAS founder Jim Goodnight's philosophy: "When everyone told Jim he needed a five-year plan, it didn't make sense to him. So we didn't do it. In the fast-changing technology industry, if you try to follow a five-year plan, your products will be irrelevant by the time they hit the market."

Avoid sweeping Destinations like "enhanced customer satisfaction." Employees have a general understanding of what this means but certainly not enough to fully get behind it and ensure that you arrive there. Again, we recommend the chunking process discussed in chapter 2. Break down customer satisfaction into its parts so that each part culminates in delivering a better customer experience, for example,

- Delivering our customer experience with every customer interaction

- Creating a loyal customer with every interaction

With this, each team meets to discuss and decide on its participation in reaching this organizational Destination. For example, actions may include

- Removing constraints to delivering customer experience

- Adopting a new scheduling program so we can work more effectively

Also, individuals' behaviors and responsibilities should align with team and organizational Destinations. Make sure everyone understands the relevance of getting there, what it means for everyone if you do get there, and the role you need each of them to play in getting there.

"Involving people gives leaders an immense self-confidence. In tackling problems, they have the perspective of many brains."

—Bob Doak, W. L. Gore & Associates, Inc.

>> *How much have you delegated the job of communicating this Destination to your organization?*

Optimum People-Profit Opportunities

Like a plane with multiple stops, you may be headed to many Destinations. We've found, though, that having more than three Destinations will make it hard to get anything done. Stay with one to three organizational Destinations at a time and chart more as you reach each one. All Destinations should culminate in using your Optimum People-Profit Opportunities (OPPOs), advancing your OPPOs, or building new OPPOs. An OPPO is whatever your organization does better than anyone else and, in your customers' minds, the experience they buy from you.

Is the customer who purchases cosmetics from Revlon buying only lipstick and blush? We think not. She's buying being more beautiful, confident, and sexy. How about the customer who buys a Harley-Davidson motorcycle? Harley riders will tell you they aren't just buying bikes. They're buying membership in an elite group. Membership is the product. If you watch closely, you will see every Harley rider give a subtle wave to all other Harley riders when they pass on the road. This is just a part of the experience you get as a Harley owner. Make sure you know what your customers are buying, as this will ensure the best leverage of your Optimum People-Profit Opportunities.

>> *What are your organization's Optimum People-Profit Opportunities? How are your employees connected to them?*

Consider the OPPOs of these leading companies. Each has found what it does best and brought in leaders who can galvanize people around their Optimum People-Profit Opportunities:

- **Southwest Airlines**—Offering freedom for people to go places and see people and do new things

- **Starbucks**—Creating a third place, after home and work, where people want to go

- **McDonald's**—Delivering a fast eating experience that the family can enjoy together

- **W. L. Gore & Associates**—Applying the polymer PTFE in innovative ways

- **Con-way**—Providing highly differentiated and innovative supply-chain solutions to the shipping public

- **SC Johnson**—Developing products that make people's lives cleaner, better, and safer

If you decide on a Destination that takes you outside your OPPO, do it thoughtfully, because the risks will be much higher and the rewards possibly much lower. Say that your Destination is to have the hottest brand for 20-somethings three years from now. But, as you look around your organization, you realize that no one is under 35, and you've never marketed to the under-35 age group. You need to ramp up your employee experience and understand your new market before you can realistically implement the Destination.

As you pursue your Destination, be sure to focus on your strengths, not on the obstacles in your way. Don't ignore the obstacles, but do give the most resources to those strengths inside your organization that will help you get to the Destination. Why? Because they are already in place, and, often, all success takes is removing some barriers and letting current strengths carry your organization forward. If you want to increase profitability from 2 to 5 percent, don't simply focus on your weaknesses or perceived constraints that may hinder you. Focus on what you have in place that could make it work instead of focusing on what you don't have. Perhaps your strengths, if enhanced, would be enough to ensure that your organization reaches the Destination. Leveraging your strengths enables better performance and is a lot more enjoyable than trying to be something you're not.

>> *What are your organization's three greatest strengths? How are you building them at every level?*

Awareness of Route Options and Diversions

Once you choose your Destination, assess where you are today and decide on the best route for getting there. If you have two Destinations, look at each, find common strengths for attaining both, and chart your course by prioritizing the steps to achieving both Destinations.

If you want to be number one in the market, and today you're number eight, what are your options for moving to number one? New products? A larger sales force? New marketplaces? New channels of distribution? Can you jump from eight to one, or is it more realistic to jump to seven first? If you think it's realistic to jump to one, build that goal into your plan. Just remember that you need to be able to sell this Destination to your employees in a way that is, and feels, realistic. Leaders always believe an organization can act more quickly than it can. The rate of progress will always be influenced by a variety of personalities and agendas.

Prepare for unexpected diversions. In an industry in which a new competitor could appear overnight or a current competitor could pull out of a market or file for bankruptcy, be ready to move fast. If you're bogged down by bureaucracy and your plan doesn't allow for unexpected diversions, you're at risk of missing your Destination.

Triple Focus on Organization, Team, and Individuals

Destination Planning has three focuses: organizational Destinations, team Destinations, and individual Destinations. Ideally, of course, all are working together and moving toward the same outcomes. That's an effective way to build an organization that delivers on its promises.

Organization Focus

At the organizational level, Destination is the big picture. The Destination shapes the vision, the overall business and strategic plans, and the hiring process. Let's take a look at three different organizational Destinations through the lens of three airlines.

Southwest Airlines set the organizational Destination of selecting the cities it would serve based on three parameters: frequency, low cost, and market impact. Over the years, it's garnered requests for airline service from many cities, along with attractive incentives from city governments. Yet the airline has never wavered from its Destination, continuing to turn down any offers that do not fit its three-point selection process.

In the mid-1990s, Continental Airlines decided to dramatically change its Destination, starting with how it did business inside. Gordon Bethune had joined Continental—against his better judgment, he says, since he "wanted to remain sane!"[1] He instantly recognized the need to implement some simple, yet clearly defined, Destinations. The teams working on Continental's turnaround had a series of meetings so they could understand why it was so difficult to get anything done inside the organization. They had great customers and great planes, but they were operating in bankruptcy.

Continental opted for the Destination "working together," which was intended to streamline everything about the airline's internal procedures. The company replaced its 880-page employee manual with an 80-page guide to getting things done. Bethune asked questions about Continental's strategic plans for the routes it was flying, most of which were randomly chosen at that time. Continental decided to fly only to places its customers wanted to go instead of to places its competitors flew or pilots recommended.

The change from copying competitors to finding a Destination inherently right for its needs turned the company around. Continental not only emerged from bankruptcy, it became known as a great workplace and appeared on *Fortune*'s Best Places to Work list for several years in a row.

JetBlue Airways was founded with a distinct organizational Destination: "Bring humanity back to air travel." Dave Neeleman, former CEO of Morris Air, wanted to turn around the industry's overall reputation for treating people poorly by serving up an incredible flying experience. He shared his 1,000-page business plan with brothers Mike Barger, a U.S. Navy pilot, and Dave Barger, vice president of operations for Continental Airlines in Newark, New Jersey. "Mike and I had been talking for years about what we could do together," Dave Barger says. "We were just at the point where we were ready to do something else when Dave Neeleman dropped the business plan on my desk."

> > *What are some Destinations you believe your organization needs to reach?*

For three days, the brothers pored over Neeleman's plan. They were excited by what they read. "We could see what he saw—a high-quality airline service with low fares that would attract a loyal market," says Barger. "It was truly an opportunity to make the world a better place, one flight at a time." The

Bargers joined Neeleman in 1999 to launch JetBlue. Today, Neeleman's ultimate organizational Destination continues to be reached every day, as JetBlue whittles away at the competition, employing more than 11,000 and serving more than 30,000 customers—and turning profits every quarter.

Team Focus

At the team level, Destination is all about how the function of the team contributes to the organization's goals. If your organization's Destination is "create outstanding customer teams" but you don't have a dedicated customer-service team, then you'd better get one! If your Destination is "be completely paperless in three years," then you can reassign your printing department.

Organizational Destinations should be on the agendas of team meetings, incorporated into team goals, continually monitored for progress, and allotted time and resources. Each time a Destination is revealed in an organization, teams need to use the start, stop, and continue strategy. That is, they need to pull the entire team together and ask what team members should start, stop, and continue doing that will lead them to the Destination in the most direct, fastest way. This assessment is critical for teams to understand their role in achieving the Destination as well as to begin making changes that result in progress.

> *"We make most of our decisions by team, so we look for people who enjoy team-based contribution."*
> —Gail Baity, Vice President of Human Resources,
> Corning Incorporated

We encourage teams to focus on what they do well in order to reach Destinations, just as they would read a map to find the best route. Deploy resources and activities that enable you to best reach your Destinations. Teams should focus on work that moves them toward organizational Destinations. All team activities must fit under some organizational Destination or contribute to the organization's overall mission. Too much leniency about teams choosing what projects to work on eventually leads to misalignment.

Individual Focus

At the individual level, the focus is on crafting employee job descriptions, annual review processes, and compensation programs that support the team Destination and, ultimately, the organizational Destination. It's also about supporting the Destinations that people set, such as better health or personal finance goals. It's in your organization's best interests to have physically and financially healthy employees as this will help them improve their performance and develop their understanding of how your organization makes money. The goal, though, while they're with you, is to move your organization closer to reaching the Destination by simply focusing their behavior and contributions toward those of the organization.

>> *Considering team performance, what Destinations might be important for you to reach?*

Needs First, Solutions Second

Remember, a key part of Awareness is that leaders know the needs of their stakeholders and then find solutions that meet those needs, as described in chapter 2. Since most customers and employees lead with a solution, we want to ensure that we are actually in the business of meeting needs.

One of our clients decided that the company had a significant problem with recognition within the organization. Leaders called on us to help with their new Destination, "implement a reward and recognition program." The people who called us were so convinced that recognition was the solution that they were already pricing gadgets and trinkets they could hand out whenever someone did something worthy of recognition.

They even paid a high-priced consulting group to design the perfect reward system, complete with point values for behaviors. It was a total flop. Why? Because the solution was launched before the need was truly understood. Employees did not want more trinkets and T-shirts proclaiming their ability to do what they were being paid to do. What they wanted was more opportunities to be included in decisions that affect the business and, more important, themselves. Since most people have learned to lead with a solution, we wanted to learn what the expected outcomes were for the organization and the employees in the reward system.

When we asked team members how they had decided on this particular program, they all replied that employees were upset and complained about wanting more recognition. The leaders interpreted recognition to mean trinkets, but the employees were really saying they wanted validation of their skills and abilities, not a reward for just doing their jobs. When we asked employees how they wanted to be recognized, they said, "by respecting us enough to know we know something!" In charting your Destination, remember that you're in the business of first understanding needs and then applying solutions.

How the Company Makes Money

Many employees don't understand their roles in making money for their company. In our work, we find that it's difficult for employees to help an organization perform when they have no idea how their organization actually makes money. It's not just for-profits we're talking about. In nonprofits, employees don't understand how their funding works; and, in government, there's this whole tax thing, but do they really understand how hard it is to create cash flow in an organization?

Think we're being dramatic? Ask any of your employees how your organization brings in cash. During one of our speaking engagements with a large retailing company, we posed the question of exactly how the company makes its money. We had hoped for answers that centered on the OPPO, the brand of the retailer, and perhaps that little-known fact that repeat buyers account for more than 50 percent of all profits.

A woman in the audience immediately raised her hand when we asked how the company made money. "We take credit cards," she said. It was not exactly the answer we were looking for, but it was a start. Someone else commented, "We sell products." The Awareness phase may reveal other unknowns for your organization. Look for them, and add them to your Destination Planning.

A Real Destination

Again, always make sure your Destination is realistic and attainable and that it's the best Destination for your business. If your employees don't feel it, they most likely can't see it, and they won't be inclined to help you get there.

One strategy is to bring together your organization's top influencers—people you can count on to make things happen—to make sure they understand your Destination, buy into it, and will help champion it. If you already know who your influencers are, you can also use this group in planning your Destination. Having early buy-in saves a lot of time in the selling and teaching phases of the Destination.

East Alabama Medical Center has traditionally conducted focus groups before announcing any organizational change or new Destination. When hospital leaders officially unveil the Destination, they're miles closer to reaching it, because people have already bought in through small-group discussions. The leadership team follows up with a communication to employees' families so as to get them on board, further connecting people to the business and reinforcing the Destination by building a wider group of stakeholders.

Reinforce the Destination continuously. Make it a part of everyday business and an instant and ongoing part of your culture —from face-to-face meetings and performance reviews to celebratory events, newsletter and intranet updates, and postings on the lunchroom wall.

When you reach each Destination, let every one of your stakeholders know. Stay in constant touch with all constituencies. How they see the organization may be different from how you see it, and their feedback can help propel you forward.

Keep in mind that different stakeholders may need different levels of detail. But make sure the picture you paint is always concrete, consistent, and compelling. The checklist in the following chart will help you address costly operating beliefs and assumptions immediately and without exception.

Your Unique Thing

The fastest way to reach a Destination is by taking the most direct and least resistant path. We've found that companies that leverage their unique culture, or their "thing," can bring people on board much faster. Harness your organization's innate culture —your employees, their experience, and their preferred way of getting things done—to your advantage.

Costly Operating Beliefs and Assumptions

Your journey to your Destination could be derailed by people's beliefs and assumptions. Here's a checklist of the most common ones.

Beware of costly operating beliefs . . .

1. The Destination isn't real. We can't get there.

2. It's the wrong Destination, and we tried it before.

3. It's another excuse to make money for management.

4. The current thinking will suffice. Do we really want to be that good?

5. This is just another fragmented attempt to turn things around.

. . . and assumptions . . .

6. The most direct route is a straight line.

7. We have enough buy-in to get this done.

8. Our workforce is ready for this Destination, and employees' roles are clear.

9. We have the infrastructure to get to this Destination.

10. We can control change. (Change may be managed intentionally, but it cannot be controlled.)

W. L. Gore, named the most innovative culture in the world by *Fast Company,* leverages its thing—innovation—to support every Destination it sets for itself. One of Gore's ongoing and most powerful Destinations is "make money and have fun." When Founder Bill Gore was alive, his business was a highly attractive acquisition target for numerous organizations. Several calls a year came in from companies that wanted to buy Gore. They all had big plans, seeking to leverage the tremendous intellectual property Gore had developed.

Bill always welcomed anyone to come talk to him about Gore; that's just the type of person he was. He asked would-be buyers what they had to contribute to Gore's success. "Money," each prospect answered. "We have lots of money to sink into your company." Bill knew that money wasn't the reason to be involved in Gore, so he told them, "Thanks, but we have enough money, and I'm having fun!" At Gore, making money results in having fun, and having fun drives more energy for making money. This beautiful pairing has been applied consistently to nearly everything that happens at Gore.

Gore has enabled itself to compete by being the world leader in polytetrafluoroethylene (PTFE) applications. The company believes so fundamentally that innovation is at the heart of its business that it's removed traditional organizational constraints such as bosses, standard compensation programs, and job descriptions. Gore also rejects official titles, based on the early philosophy that if you give people a title, it assumes they have automatic authority. At Gore, you're a leader only when you have followers. The company doesn't use words like *have to* and *permission*. Who has time for that type of hierarchy when you want to be innovative? We agree!

The most direct route for Gore is to work in small teams and keep production teams to no more than 200 people. It would be much less expensive for Gore to use huge plants that would cut pure cost, but it doesn't. Why? Because leaders realize that once you have a team with a lot more people, it becomes harder to develop the relationships needed to be effective. Size has an impact on communication, interactions, and the ability to influence. Since Gore has no official titles, you really do need to know who everyone is if you intend to get things done. The company believes that smaller work groups provide bigger opportunities to tap into people's ideas for innovation.

How can you know that your organization is going in the right direction? Use the questions in Exercise 4, on page 134, to guide you.

SEI Investments' unique formula, their thing, for winning in the marketplace is high-performing teams. The company has gone to great lengths to help teams do everything together. When a team is working on a project, team members don't go to a conference room. They wheel their desks, along with their phones and computers, connected to cords in the ceiling, to their meeting place and stay together until the project is finished.

SC Johnson has a very clear reason for being in business: The company believes it exists for the greater good of the world. Does that include making money? Absolutely. But SC Johnson comes to work each day not only to produce great products but to make the world a better place. That philosophy is imparted to every one of the company's 12,000 people.

> *"Our company seeks that special combination of winning and doing the right thing, both—not winning at the expense of doing the right thing."*
>
> —Karen Ferraro, Director of Americas and Corporate Human Resources, SC Johnson

Karen Ferraro, director of Americas and corporate HR, talks about first coming to work at SC Johnson, when she sat in business meetings and constantly interjected her thoughts on the effect each business decision might have on the company's people. However, she quickly realized that she didn't need to bring it up all the time, because whenever SCJ talks about the business, the company of course means the people.

Exercise (4)

DO WE HAVE THE RIGHT DESTINATION
FOR OUR UNIQUE CULTURE?

These questions—and your answers—can serve as guideposts as you determine your organization's short-term Destinations and ultimate Destination.

1. Who will celebrate this Destination with us when we
    achieve it?

2. How will this Destination truly contribute to the
    organization?

3. How will achieving this Destination solve a problem for
    our primary customers?

4. Do the short-term checkpoints support the intended
    Destination?

5. If circumstances require a change, do we have an
    alternate route?

6. Who specifically is being served with this Destination?

7. What value will this Destination add to our employees?

8. Why are we doing this now?

9. How long will it take us to arrive at this Destination?

10. When will we know we've arrived at our intended Destination?

The idea of SAS Institute began one night with a diagram on the back of a cocktail napkin and the philosophy of building a place where people are treated well. The cocktail napkin sketch, shown in Figure 3, grew into a customer value proposition, with two parts and four points.

SAS's treatment of its customers mirrors the company's treatment of its employees. The business model and the employee model both emphasize investing in long-term relationships in order to drive returns and build a profitable organization for the long run.

No Guarantee with First to Market

If you listened to what they told you in business school, getting to market first is the best Destination. Yet, growing evidence indicates that being first to market doesn't guarantee long-term dominance. Instead of blindly following textbook advice, be sure to focus on what will actually work for your unique organization.

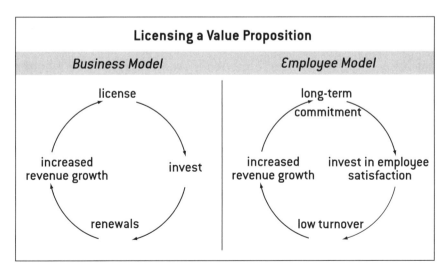

Figure 3. The SAS Value Proposition

SC Johnson wasn't the first to come on the market with household products. But, today, they're number one or number two in every market they target. Chux's Diapers was the first disposable diaper but Pampers dominates now. Books.com had 400,000 titles on the Internet before Amazon.com took over. WebVan was the first grocery delivery system; now FreshDirect has pulled ahead, while WebVan has closed its doors. There are numerous other examples of companies whose Destination was "first to market" but who now wish they had waited to enter that particular market space. Why? Because others who were better prepared swooped in and took over the market space of the first-to-market provider.

Do you remember Trommer's Red Letter? Probably not; probably now you buy market leader Miller Lite beer. But, Miller wasn't first. How about Magnavox Odyssey? You've certainly heard of the dominant player in videogames, Sony PlayStation. However, Magnavox Odyssey was in the videogame business long before Sony. White Castle was selling hamburgers, known as Sliders, back in 1921 and is recognized as the first fast-food chain, decades before the golden arches of McDonald's appeared.

We're not saying that first to market is a bad place to be; certainly, it worked for Coca-Cola. If everything else in your organization is aligned and you're first to market, you do have a better chance of pulling ahead of your competitors. A better Destination, though, might be "first to differentiate," because it's a Destination with long-term sustainability. However, that in and of itself is not a sustainable Destination. Your organization must be better than others at adapting to changing consumer preferences. Adapting might include being first to market, but it might not. This is why it's so critical to choose your Destinations strategically, in a meaningful and focused way, always looking for the long-term sustainable advantage.

For more tips on a successful journey to your Destination, see the tips on pages 137–138.

Getting There: Tips for an On-Time Arrival

---

1. Do a ground check. Fix any problems in your organization that could divert you from your Destination. For example, if people distrust leadership, you'll have a hard time selling your Destination. Address the problem before you try to introduce something new.

2. Take a number, please. We've found that what's measured usually gets done. Find a metric that will make your Destination specific and attainable—for example, "We will reach our Destination of improved profitability when our profits increase 25 percent next year," or "We will consider ourselves a great workplace when 85 percent of our people define us that way."

3. Watch your radar. Always keep track of your competitors because their Destinations will help inform yours. If you and your competitors are headed to the same Destination, you don't necessarily have to get there first. First isn't always best. Take the route that makes the most sense for your organization, not theirs.

4. Execute with focus. Executing with focus is getting the right things done, and doing them at the right time to move your business forward. It's stopping projects that don't make sense and pursuing only those that are connected to your ultimate Destination. Execute the trajectory between where you are today and where you can be tomorrow. Use the model of "think and do," making sure you have sufficient resources, commitment, and focus.

5. Mark the milestones. A good pilot notes progress along the way. When you reach a milestone—for example, a product launch—acknowledge, celebrate, and reward it. Success builds success. Recognition does much to infuse people with the energy they need to stay the course.

Getting There: Tips for an On-Time Arrival (continued)

6. Stay transparent. Transparency about a Destination indicates that you believe the Destination is the right one and will likely bring success. It may feel risky to be open about it, but it also helps people feel they're on board and collectively accountable for reaching the goal. If you need to change the route, announce the change, explain the thinking behind it, and describe what needs to happen next.

7. Be resilient. Few journeys are completely smooth. Teaching people in your organization to be resilient will help you persevere. Highly resilient people can adapt and thrive better during nonstop change. They read new situations rapidly, rebound from setbacks, adapt quickly, and stay engaged under constant pressure.

If you can help people see the Destination from the start, and feel the importance of their place on the flight, they'll be happy to stay on board. When we feel it, we give it. That's what Awareness is all about.

(5) ALIGNMENT

*Charting the Course
to Your Destination*

You've chosen your Destination. Now you need to get everyone and everything working toward it. Alignment is the map that charts your course.

In Alignment, you make sure that your people, processes, and systems are all headed in the same direction, one that supports your Destination. Alignment involves the entire structure of your organization from top to bottom, as well as your employees' connection to customers, which enhances their ability to provide each customer with the best experience possible.

In fact, you can get a good indication of whether a company is aligned by experiencing its customer service. If a customer calls and is routed to 15 or so people to get a question answered, you know you're misaligned. Customers should be able to talk to one person in the organization who can meet all their needs. Great alignment leads to great service.

How can FedEx assure you, with complete confidence, that it will deliver a package overnight to most locations in the world, but many airlines can't seem to get your luggage 400 miles, from point A to point B? What enables Lands' End to remember your last order, while credit card companies still send you applications even though you've been carrying their cards for years? The answer is astoundingly simple: Some companies are aligned, and others operate like many smaller separate organizations under the same company name.

> >> List every point of contact a customer has with
>   your organization. Which department is responsible
>   for serving each of these points of contact?

When your leadership team sets the company's Destination, take a close look at every area of your organization. See what's aligned and what isn't. Target your misalignments and create a plan to resolve them.

Aligning your organization ultimately comes down to balancing priorities, eliminating mixed messages, determining values, identifying and removing constraints, and designing systems that support reaching a shared Destination. The ability to do this is a powerful contribution to all stakeholders and can eliminate virtually millions of customer frustrations. Aligned organizations are a significant threat to competitors, as the entire organization, not just those on the front lines of customer service, is aligned around the customer.

"Our perspective is we're all rowing together. We want everybody to be rowing in the same direction."

—Gail Baity, Vice President of Human Resources, Corning Incorporated

Out of Sync

Alignment may seem a daunting task. But a misaligned organization costs more to operate. Inefficiencies create excess in an organization, in the forms of increased inventory, costs, and waste. Employee turnover is higher because people can't do what they do best, and productivity is lower because it takes much longer to get anything done. People stop developing and engaging because the culture is dysfunctional. Customers are inconvenienced, and inconvenienced customers eventually quit being customers.

Misalignment can happen at the individual, team, and organizational levels and in every aspect of the organization—priorities, resources, leadership, expectations, rewards and reprimands, training and motivation, and, of course, culture. If your Optimum People-Profit Opportunity (OPPO) is new product development, but you have a low-trust risk-averse culture, you're out of sync. Developing products is all about trying new things and taking risks. A culture that doesn't support risk-taking will be very costly as you move toward your Destination.

Scott directly experienced individual misalignment: In the early 1980s, he was fired from his job at McDonald's after he got a little too creative with the condiments. Scott's mind-set was totally misaligned with McDonald's nonnegotiables, one of which is that every customer at every McDonald's around the world should receive a consistent product. Scott had a creative vision for how the hamburgers should look—a vision that included making smiley faces with the ketchup and mustard. Management was much less thrilled than Scott with the "smiley burger"! And imagine if your fish sandwich arrived arrayed with pickles, one of Scott's favorites!

Since having Scott cook the food was not working out, he was moved to the counter, to take customers' orders. Unfortunately, given his propensity to engage in conversation, he spent an extraordinary amount of time talking to customers—undercutting the "fast" part of the fast-food concept. In hindsight, McDonald's did the right thing in letting Scott go. It's in the company's best interest to hire people who understand the Destinations of consistency and efficiency and can adapt to and work in a rules-based environment.

> > *What are the characteristics of your organization's most successful employees? How do these traits fit into your hiring and recruiting plan? How does your organization give feedback or coaching using these characteristics as examples of excellence?*

Misalignment is often found between departments. What happens when marketing launches a direct-mail campaign for a new service, but customer service knows nothing about it when the calls start pouring in? What happens when sales promises a new product to customers right before the holiday season, but operations can't make the product in time? When one group makes promises that are not aligned with what another group can do, everyone has to scramble to make it work, or the company will break its promise to customers. The scramble is not an effective method for Alignment because it builds resentment and eventually creates the need for one department to circumvent another in order to get its needs met.

> > *What do you do to ensure alignment in each department? Which departments are at odds with one another? How might you reorganize your organization to align these departments?*

Aligned businesses report results, not just busyness. If you see a lot of busy people, with meetings and jobs that are full of activity, you can bet there's misalignment guiding much of their work. No one wants to look incompetent, so the day is full of things to do, but not necessarily the right things. How do we know what the right things are? For that, we need to be clear on the Destinations and be able to link our work to reaching them.

A Shared Mind-Set for Aligning the Organization

If they are to reach Destinations, organizations need to make sure everyone is headed in the same direction. Instead of simply reacting to any issue that emerges and making sudden shifts, aligned organizations are strong enough to perform regardless of what's happening in the world around them. Being an aligned organization is a shared mind-set that purposefully shapes people, their behavior, their outputs, and the entire organization's focus on arriving at the Destination.

Have you ever wondered why most employees come to work each day instead of working in their homes? People are together in an organization so that they can get things done. If there were no inherent reason for us to be in the same building, then we should all work from home and do our own thing! If we're going to go to the expense of having a place where we do business together and building systems that enable us to communicate, we need to leverage this time and culture to make things happen. People working together is one of the strongest elements in creating a shared mind-set and making sure the organization is driven to its highest performance levels.

People are most likely to support what they create. Therefore, we recommend asking questions and getting people involved during the first few steps of Alignment. For example, let's listen in on this conversation between Christopher, a senior leader, and Gordon, a line manager:

Christopher: Hi, Gordon. Do you have a minute?

Gordon: Absolutely.

Christopher: Remember last month we gathered input for how we were going to expand sales of all our latest products by 20 percent, with special focus on broadening Target and Wal-Mart?

Gordon: I remember; it sounds like a great idea.

Christopher: Yes, it's a Destination we all can work toward together. What questions do you have about this goal?

Gordon: None, really, other than when we want to actually achieve it.

Christopher: Excellent question. We hope to have the shelf space added by this time next year.

Gordon: Yes, we talked about that quite a bit, but I didn't really have any ideas for making that happen. I'm not in sales or marketing.

Christopher: That's exactly why your perspective is so important. If we were to actually get to that 20 percent increase, what do you think would need to happen inside our company?

Gordon: The first thing is to make sure we have enough people to make more products. Then, we need to work on the packaging for nearly everything we make because we use a color that's customized just for us. The number one reason we ship late is that we never have enough packaging!

Christopher: That's great to know. Maybe we can speak with operations to figure out that color issue. Anything else that might need to be tweaked?

As this conversation shows, asking questions while you chart the course to your Destination enables you to garner valuable information and insight from those involved and uncover any areas that are misaligned. Typically, those closest to the actual work have better ideas on how to get to the Destination.

W. L. Gore & Associates strives to align its 7,000 people by lining up the values of the company with the values of the individual and taking the extra step to tie in the rationale of the decision. It consistently takes the approach of "Tell me why this is the right thing to do," says CEO Terri Kelly. "If you believe something is the right thing to do, you'll be a lot more energized to do it because you personally buy into it."

> *"This is the alignment—tying decisions to*
> *company values and gaining buy-in from*
> *associates—that makes us money."*
>
> —Terri Kelly, CEO, W. L. Gore & Associates, Inc.

W. L. Gore's culture of inclusiveness and involvement makes a big difference in how it does business. While many hierarchical organizations believe that inclusiveness is frustrating, reaching decisions through consensus produces a tremendous dynamic. For example, when you reach a decision that all employees support because they were included in the decision-making, that aligns people to the organization. The business results are dramatic.

Organizations often believe that consensus-seeking or inclusiveness will lead to never making decisions. Yet we've found that aligned and inclusive organizations need to make fewer decisions because the ones they do make are supported by their people. This also enables them to rely less on systems to make things happen.

SC Johnson was one of the first companies to provide child care centers for its employees. Although it's not unusual for SCJ to be first in workplace trends, the company's leadership is gifted at recognizing and responding to employee needs. Leaders at SC Johnson realized that even though the child care center was going to be a welcome addition, without expansion there might be a waiting list for employees who wanted to enroll their children at the center. The year SCJ decided to open the facility was also a softer economic year for the company, but the Johnsons decided to undertake a $5 million expansion of the center anyway; they didn't feel it was consistent with "This We Believe," the SC Johnson values statement, to have some employees on a waiting list.

While some stakeholders were worried about the decision, especially given the economic environment, it was only necessary to say that the decision was consistent with "This We Believe." Immediately, alignment was generated throughout the organization.

While the addition to the child care center was being constructed, the only building close enough to house the children was a church. But it didn't have air conditioning. Again, driven by "This We Believe," SCJ realized that it only made sense to equip the church with air conditioning. Leaders of SC Johnson could have looked at this as an expense, but they didn't. They looked at who they were as a company, and, when they did, the course of action was obvious.

Team Alignment

The senior leadership team evaluates the entire organization, but departments and teams need to look at themselves to make sure their efforts are aligned with the organization's Destination. Mid-level managers hold the power to align team members with the Destination and support them in driving the Destination forward.

Given that most organizations are structured in parts—departments of expertise, from marketing to HR to R&D—we need to find ways to connect them in an ongoing and focused way. You may have an amazing product or a terrific marketing department, but if operations can't make the product quickly enough to supply demand, everyone loses. An organization is only as strong as its weakest part.

In many companies today, departments compete instead of working together. Maybe marketing competes with sales over who gets credit. Or departments may be working toward different goals. We believe that aligned organizations have departments and teams whose mind-set is to serve one another, with the ultimate goal of together serving the customer.

With alignment, "we" and "they" become "us." If we don't all share the same map, each department or unit may take a different route based on its needs. As a result, it's easy to diverge and even get lost.

>> *What incentives are in place to reward collaboration across departments? What departments are the most aligned today in your organization? Why?*

Let's consider, for example, a misaligned HR and legal department. HR is charged with recruiting the best talent and onboarding the new hires successfully. During hiring, HR sends a letter of employment drafted by legal welcoming the new person to the organization. Yet the "welcome letter" is often full of legal jargon that confuses the person who receives it instead of making him or her feel welcomed. This is a minor, yet real, example of misalignment. If both HR and legal were to adopt the same Destination of "welcoming new hires," they could work together to find language that addresses the legal issues in a warmer manner.

Still, even well-aligned organizations miss the mark every now and then. Several years ago the marketing team at Southwest Airlines launched a systemwide $25 sale on flights to most of its destinations. For competitive reasons, details were shared with only a few key people. Unfortunately, customer service and reservation agents did not have adequate preparation time, and when the promotion launched, it nearly shut down the system. Customers called and came, only to find that the phone lines were jammed and counter waiting lines were long.

Although marketing had a clear Destination—to fill seats—the Destination wasn't defined for other departments. Southwest learned that alignment is making sure that everyone who's going to be affected by a decision is informed of and engaged in the process.

It's easier to be aligned when you're a smaller organization, but size should never be an excuse for misalignment. Take it department by department, team by team. And keep your teams small. As Jeff Bezos of Amazon.com said, it's best to limit the size of a team to the number of people who can be fed with two pizzas! That way, you can make continuous small adjustments as you move forward. As you reach one Destination and another appears, teams can work through the Alignment process quickly and conscientiously, reshift and reorganize priorities, and adopt the behaviors needed to reach the new Destination. They stop what they no longer need to do and continue—or start—what they do need to do.

>> *How do you measure alignment in your organization?*

Alignment for Individuals

We're talking about hiring as well as value descriptions and contribution evaluations for aligning individuals in your organization. Since some of these terms may be unfamiliar ones for people-profit connections, we'll look at them more closely.

Hiring

Hiring for your Optimum People-Profit Opportunity is key to an aligned organization. If, for example, your OPPO is developing products faster than any of your competitors, you'll want to factor that competency into every person you hire. You'll want to avoid hiring candidates who are successful overall but are not poised for success in your organization because their skills are misaligned with your Destination.

When a popular cookie franchise first opened stores in a new region, it hired store managers first and gave them the autonomy to hire their own people for their own stores. Once hires were completed, corporate headquarters monitored each of the new stores. It found that some stores were generating profits and sales in alignment with company expectations, but one particular store was not. One advantage of operating a franchise is that the corporation has spent time developing your business plan for you; they know what works and what doesn't. They can project store earnings very closely based on the demographics of the area.

When corporate headquarters investigated this low-performing store, it realized the franchise's hiring practices weren't aligned with company expectations. When the manager was hired, she placed ads in local venues touting such enticements as "New start-up in the area. Be an entrepreneur. Come and try new things." She interviewed for the skills required to be entrepreneurial, not those needed to follow the business plan for a franchise. Bringing in people who liked to try new things wasn't in alignment with an organization that needed people to "follow the rules exactly as written" in setting up the business for success.

Southwest is well known for its practice of hiring for attitude and training for skills. The company often uses employees and even customers in the selection process—a kind of built-in assurance that those who are hired are aligned with the values and spirit of Southwest's culture.

JetBlue Airways hires people "for their heart," says Mike Barger. "We look for people who fit with our values-based decision-making culture—people with the passion to take care of people." The company realizes that the JetBlue experience isn't for everyone. "It doesn't mean you're a bad person," Barger says. "It just means you'll need to find someplace else to be great."

> *"I can teach anyone to fly an Airbus A320. But I can't tell them how to be nice. That needs to come from inside."*
>
> —Captain Mike Barger, Vice President and
> Chief Learning Officer, JetBlue Airways

SC Johnson looks for people who can live the values of its core operating guidelines, the document called "This We Believe." "It was put together in 1976, well before mission and vision statements came into vogue," says Kelly Semrau, vice president of global public affairs and communication. "It's our moral compass and a map for how we operate. People we hire need to get that at the business, intellectual, and emotional levels."

Value Descriptions and Contribution Evaluations

Instead of crafting job descriptions for individuals, we advocate creating value descriptions. Tell people the value of executing on your organizational Destinations and customer experience.

Traditional job descriptions often have nothing to do with the jobs or the people we try to cram into them. They put people in boxes and frequently do more to create a cycle of mistrust. You don't want to hire, interview, and rate people based on job descriptions that tell them what to do but leave out why their jobs are important. Tell them why those jobs matter, the value they bring to the organization and, yes, even the world. Remember, everyone wants to make a major difference to the organization, to the team, and to themselves!

We've never met a job description we really liked, and we've never met a performance review we really liked, either. The traditional end-of-the-year evaluations based on performance don't seem to work in an organization striving for alignment. These evaluations typically don't reflect the contributions of the individual, the potential of the teams, or the needs of the customer. When the performance review doesn't factor in the customer experience and what the customer is paying you for, your evaluation process is bound to be misaligned.

People need to understand how their jobs are connected to helping the organization reach its Destination; they can then be evaluated specifically on their contributions. If your Destination is to be number one in the market, but your review process focuses only on things that you think are important but have no direct tie-in to reaching that Destination, it's a costly misalignment. If you evaluate your executive assistant on being on time every day and creating an effective filing system, but not on contributions he or she has made to help your organization get to number one, you're not aligning that person's contribution with the collective Destination.

A Destination Champion

Achieving alignment is a major undertaking. It involves setting time frames, coordinating teams and individuals who are working together, ensuring that all behaviors and activities are consistent with the Destination, creating the best sequence of events and conversations, and removing any obstacles that get in the way.

We've found that an effective strategy for securing alignment is to designate a Destination Champion, or DC. We think of the DC as an air traffic controller, with the vantage point of seeing the entire organization clearly—up, down, and across—and the responsibility of overseeing each participant's safe take-off and landing (see Figure 4). The DC can serve as a central hub in coordinating a web of relationships, monitoring constraints, ensuring communication among departments, creating checkpoints for progress, and fostering a broader sense of shared identity and vision, especially when groups are divided. The DC can also create opportunities for collective actions.

Once you've set your Destination, the DC should schedule a meeting with all department heads, whether or not they will have direct impact on the Destination. Often, the legal department, or the HR department, might not be included in plans for customer-related Destinations. By excluding departments, however, we

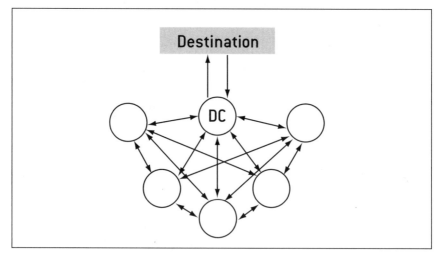

Figure 4. The Destination Champion

open up the risk that they will not understand, and therefore will not support, reaching the Destination. Plus, they may have a valuable perspective that we didn't see.

>> *Who in your organization would be an ideal Destination Champion? (Make a list and keep it for use when needed.) What support might your DC need to execute change?*

The goal of these initial meetings is to get department heads the information they need to support and align their influence, resources, and strategies toward the Destination. This will look different depending on the departments, but every department must be included, as each can assist you in some way. You also want to discuss how often department leaders would like updates on the Destination and what they should do if they have questions. Offer to meet with their teams, or send them a ready-to-go presentation on the Destination to share with their teams. Define exactly what their roles are in achieving the Destination, and emphasize the importance of their contributions.

>> *With which senior leaders might you need to work most closely to ensure that the Destination happens? That is, how do you remove any constraints to change?*

The Look of an Aligned Organization

In an aligned organization, it's easy to do business. Communication is open, transparent, and interactive. People build off one another's successes and consistently think of how they can advance toward the Destination the leadership team has set for the organization. Employees are connected to customers and understand the customers' needs so well that they constantly think of new ways to enhance and deliver on the customer experience. Any constraints to performance have been dealt with or removed, freeing the organization to do what it does best.

Southwest has mastered the art of Alignment. The company can turn a plane around in less than 20 minutes, using less people than its competitors. Employees are all working toward the same Destination and understand their role in achieving it. Southwest employees know how many people it takes per plane for them to make a profit and how many minutes a plane can sit at the gate before it begins to cost them money.

JetBlue has aligned its entire organization with a core set of values. "We don't have a 2,000-page volume of thou shalt nots," VP and Chief Learning Officer Mike Barger says. "We have more of a values-based decision-making culture, where the questions we ask our crew members to ask themselves when they're making a decision are, first, is what I'm about to do safe? If it's safe, is what I'm about to do caring? If it's caring, does what I'm about to do support our integrity? Are we telling the truth? If we are doing that, and we have a good time doing that, then it's fun to share our experiences with people. That leads to a really impassioned commitment to do it all over again."

According to Barger, JetBlue's five values of safety, caring, integrity, fun, and passion have been infused into the company's entire way of doing things—from screening, interviewing, and selecting its people, to training and operations. Aligning new hires with these core values is particularly critical during orientation, because the company hires many employees from within the industry who need to be introduced to the JetBlue point of view.

JetBlue's goal is to provide a seamless JetBlue experience for its customers at every touch point. The company strives to define the customer experience from beginning to end to make sure its workforce is aligned with this ultimate organizational Destination. Since every JetBlue employee is a crew member of some sort, every-one either touches a customer directly or touches someone who touches a customer. In fact, those are the two basic job descriptions at JetBlue: those who help passengers and those who help the ones who are helping passengers! That's an excellent Alignment tool, as it helps crew members always remember what to do!

The company has arranged its infrastructure and compensation system thoughtfully. JetBlue leaders have built an organization that can perform during economic downturns as well as times of abundance. As a result, JetBlue has never had a layoff. Because leadership firmly believes that the people side and the business side are one and the same, the company focuses on helping crew members understand why taking good care of customers is so important to economic survival.

"In orientation, we talk about the importance of repeat business and customers who have a good experience with us," Barger says. "We explain our compensation system and how it's built to survive the toughest of times in the industry and the economy. And we don't do it on the backs of our workforce. What we do is build a guaranteed compensation plan that we know we can sustain, along with a very aggressive profit-sharing and stock purchase plan for crew members."

JetBlue has also been masterful at aligning with like-minded business partners. The airline decided not to provide meals for its customers because "we don't feel airline food is any good," Mike Barger says. Instead, the company's philosophy has been to create an environment in airport terminals that provides many opportunities to purchase delicious food. JetBlue looks for food-service partners who are aligned with its goal of providing an extraordinary experience for its customers and gets them to open up shop in the places JetBlue serves. Customers are actively encouraged to buy food at the terminals and bring it onto the planes; JetBlue provides the drinks and cleans up after the meals. Staying out of the food business is good business for the airline. It lets the company focus on what it does best and enables JetBlue to stay aligned with its OPPO!

> > *What are the five most common customer complaints about your organization? How many complaints might be caused by misalignment?*

Federal Express has a quality improvement program that focuses on 12 Service Quality Indicators, or SQIs, that set high standards for service and customer satisfaction. Measuring themselves against a 100 percent standard, teams strive to improve all aspects of the way FedEx does business. Every morning at 10 a.m., managers across the FedEx world receive the SQI report. It's an instant measure of how the organization is performing, and it's an extraordinary Alignment tool. If any misalignment is found, leaders can respond to it right away.

East Alabama Medical Center uses a gain-sharing program that ties core compensation into how well the hospital performs. Yes, this is profit sharing for a nonprofit; we love paradigm breakers! "We measure performance through such metrics as patient satisfaction, clinical quality, and financial outcomes," says EAMC CEO Terry Andrus.

> *"Gain-sharing helps our people pull together*
> *and focus on what's most important."*
> —Terry Andrus, CEO, East Alabama Medical Center

Wal-Mart aligns its employees with daily updates and goal-setting sessions. Each shift at every one of the company's stores, clubs, and distribution centers starts with a storewide meeting. Here, managers discuss the daily sales figures, company news, and goals for the day with hourly associates. Meetings are punctuated by the now-famous Wal-Mart cheer, started by Wal-Mart founder Sam Walton in 1975 as a way of encouraging team spirit.

>> *Where would employees say there is alignment in their teams?*

Leaders with Followership

Alignment can happen only with leadership that has earned followers. Says Terri Kelly, CEO of W. L. Gore, "Let's say we want to establish a team, and we believe there is someone who would be an appropriate business leader for that business unit. It doesn't take a lot of time for individuals who will be part of that leader's team to come forth and say, 'I don't support that person as my leader.' We would never try to force-fit someone into a leadership role if there isn't a clear majority of followers." Leaders must do more than focus on the product; they must focus on the people who are focusing on the products.

EAMC's Andrus builds followership by coming in early every morning and making the rounds, stopping to visit with staff and taking time to listen to their concerns. As a result, he's on a first-name basis with most of the medical center's 1,800 employees. "Corporate America forgets that people in the trenches doing the real work want their leaders to be visible," he says. "Interacting every day reinforces the powerful message that those at the top really care about them."

Even when leadership is given by title or rank, it's never real until it's earned. Leadership is not an art or a science. It is, however, about concern for people and getting those people to have concern for the customers. There are fewer to-dos in leadership and a longer list of don't-dos. Leadership is the result of building strong relationships with people, giving them a Destination to strive for, and offering them a workplace that enables them to do their best work.

Think of all the historical lessons we know about leaders who led people to do terrible things. Were they unusual in the way they led? Not really. Most people are looking for leadership, and when a strong leader comes along, they follow. Leadership is a universal need in any organization. If you want to make a significant contribution as a leader, you must be able to

- **Execute:** Relentlessly get things done, regardless of constraints, resources, or time.

- **Feel and show genuine passion:** Believe what you feel and communicate it. Followers reject mediocrity in every way.

- **Listen:** Actively engage and listen to your people and your customers and use their input to make collaborative decisions.

- **Create followers:** Provide a healthy pressure to perform; tap the potential of all the people in your organization, enabling them to be who they are and do what they do best.

We've all had good and bad managers. But what is it about the ones you would follow no matter what? As we discussed this book, we pondered two managers. One manager was an exceptional doer who seemed able to accomplish things despite great odds. She was consistent and observant, and, when it came time to execute, she was absolutely brilliant. When you met with her, regardless of the agenda, you would leave thinking, "Wow, she was totally amazing." At another company, another manager was equally as good at getting things done. When you met with her, you would leave thinking, "Wow, am I ever amazing!" Both managers were good, but the second one could transfer her power into us. This kind of leader not only helps us align with a Destination but also helps us feel excited about being part of it.

> >> Who are your organization's most effective leaders? What characteristics or competencies make them so effective? Do you hire for these same competencies? Do leaders get feedback based on them?

A Constant Eye on the Competition

In the 1980s, U.S. carmakers had a goal of reducing the numbers of cars that didn't pass new-car quality inspections from 6,000 per 100,000 to 1,000 per 100,000. Just one problem: Toyota's rejection rate was already less than 50 per 100,000! Good Destination, but it wasn't aligned to aggressively advance and compete with other automakers. Therefore, it wasn't a Destination people could rally around. Certainly, the Destination was better than the stagnant quo, but it would have left U.S. automakers still far behind their competition. Here, we would have strongly recommended that the Destination be set at a rate lower than Toyota's, with higher quality goals set as they progressed.

Discount merchandiser Kmart, founded in 1952, was once the number one retailer in the United States and later found itself struggling to find its niche and distinguish itself from competitors Wal-Mart and Target, who were also launched that same year. While Wal-Mart was identified with "low prices always," Target developed an identity as a stylish trendsetter. Over the years, Wal-Mart and Target have thrived, but Kmart has had trouble adapting to the evolving marketplace.

When Kmart deviated from its core business of discount retailing and absorbed other businesses, it created misalignment in the organization's focus. By the time it realized it was misaligned,

Wal-Mart and Target had pulled way ahead. The company tried to realign by selling off its acquisitions, such as Borders Books and Sports Authority, and finding new management. It even went so far as to bring back the Blue Light Special—one of the long-term traditions of the Kmart shopping experience.

The Importance of the Experience

The ultimate payoff of an aligned organization? Your employees are connected to the business, and the business is connected to your customers. You'll be able to give your employees more than jobs to come to each day, and you'll be offering your customers more than products or services. You'll give them a great experience! Employees and customers who have great experiences always come back for more and, in the process, bring new customers to you. An aligned company is also just better equipped to move toward its Destination because the focus is clear, the path is outlined, and the goal is a collective one that everyone works toward.

As Data Return knows, an organization's way of doing business internally is often a major factor in another company's decision to do business with it. Data Return beat out 12 competitors for a prestigious account with Harvard Business Press. The reason, CLO Rand Stagen explains, was clarity of culture. "When we tell a client that we exist to improve the lives of people who use technology, it makes a significant difference. They understand that we have a nonfinancial reason for being, and this is a great attraction for current and new clients."

[6] ACCOUNTABILITY

Empowering through a Shared Purpose

You've figured out where your organization is going. Your resources are aligned to get you there. Now, in Accountability, you make it happen!

Accountability is holding the organization—including leaders, teams, and individuals—accountable for reaching the Destination. Leaders have a clear understanding of where the organization is going and demonstrate their willingness to pilot the journey. Senior leaders and managers do whatever it takes to give people a sense of ownership—to resolve issues, to speak up, to identify constraints, and to take responsibility for their shared and individual contributions. Teams understand how their responsibilities contribute to the end goal and work with other teams to strengthen their efforts. Individual employees are empowered through shared purpose and are held accountable not through control but through inspiration, dedication, and commitment. In other words, everyone commits to making it happen!

Most people who have entered the workforce in the past 15 years are averse to being controlled. Forcing people into compliance may have worked in the past, but it's no longer a viable option for companies that want to create something special for their employees and, ultimately, their customers.

Instead of compliance, leaders need to cultivate commitment. The more you foster commitment rather than force compliance, the faster you'll make it to the final step of the 4-A Process, Adaptation.

Organizations foster commitment by paying people to share their thoughts with leaders instead of just saying what the leaders want to hear. Every employee needs to think critically and to see the other side, even if it's an unpleasant experience. As we've pointed out, every time someone tells leaders only what they want to hear, everybody loses, and more often than not, an opportunity to learn something valuable flies out the window.

Accountability is an ongoing balancing act of having conversations and gauging progress. It's about getting someone to make the commitment to do something and then follow it through to completion. At W. L. Gore & Associates, when you make a commitment, it doesn't necessarily mean you have to do the work; you just agree to ensure that it gets done. That way, if you're delayed, you can ask for help and still honor your commitment.

>> *How do you cultivate commitment? Are your employees encouraged to think critically?*

No More Excuses, No More Blaming

For many organizations, accountability can be a source of value. A culture that is built around performance has built-in accountability because it consistently looks for ways of generating progress. When progress is made, the accomplishment is rewarded. And when progress is delayed, it's noticed, discussed, and dealt with immediately.

During this phase, you can expect a variety of excuses to emerge from managers about why something didn't get done. You may hear that someone was too busy, or didn't get the memo, or got it but didn't read it. Excuses will show a wide range of creativity and rationale and must be worked through swiftly and effectively.

In Accountability, all people in the organization need to make and keep their commitments, without exception. Employees must understand that missing deadlines, missing checkpoints, or taking detours from the route toward the Destination slows progress for everyone. While the employee may have a good excuse, we would suggest that Destination-reaching is just too important to tolerate excuses. If excuses are tolerated, they'll quickly become a norm in your organization. And if you tolerate some excuses but not others, Alignment begins to crumble. The best strategy in the Accountability phase is no tolerance for missed steps and extreme praise for progress. We understand that no one is perfect, yet we must strive for a sense of urgency and teamwork so that the team intervenes long before an excuse has to be used.

Excuses usually come with a good dose of blaming, which is of value to no one. The key is to build a culture that looks out for every part of the organization, including deadlines and the individuals responsible for meeting them. Unfortunately, recent and ongoing corporate scandals indicate that we've learned how to do business by accusing others rather than taking responsibility for our own actions.

> > *Does your organization have a zero-tolerance policy for excuses? How do you praise progress made toward reaching your Destination?*

Does this sound familiar? A catalog mailing has gone out late. The mailroom manager says it was the marketing manager's fault because the catalog was delivered a week later than expected. The marketing manager blames it on the graphic designer because he sent it to the printer late. The graphic designer blames the copywriter because her copy was late. The copywriter blames the operations manager for not giving her the information she needed for the new products. And so on and so on.

It's easy to get caught up in blaming because that's the easiest way out of conflict. It enables people to keep the constant pressure to perform on someone else, instead of on themselves. It's easier to point to people who aren't doing their jobs than it is to look at ourselves and see how we could maximize our contributions. A blaming culture is costly. If blaming is tolerated, it will quickly become the preferred way of handling all mistakes en route to the Destination and will stand in the way of reaching it.

> > *Is your culture a blaming one? If it is, what can you do to relaunch your culture?*

When it comes to Accountability, it's essential for everyone to accept responsibility for his or her part in a failure. By doing so, individuals and teams can quickly recognize problems, correct them, and continue moving forward, even stronger than before, toward the Destination.

We suggest a cultural relaunch, one that revitalizes your culture so that it is oriented toward contributions rather than blaming. If your Destination is to be number one or number two in your market, you'll never get there by blaming other functions for their inability to deliver. Instead of pointing fingers, point out things that are right. Use the 4-A Process to refocus your organization on a different way of doing business. Then, when you've created a contribution-oriented culture, you can use the 4-As again to reach your new Destination of top market share.

> *"At SAS, you learn by example. If you do*
> *something outside of our culture, people*
> *will let you know—kindly, but clearly—*
> *that's not the way we do business here."*
>
> —John Dornan, Manager of Corporate
> Public Relations, SAS Institute

When your employees put more emphasis on high performance than they do on making excuses or blaming, you'll know you've succeeded in Accountability.

A Healthy Pressure to Perform

Accountability is about pure performance, about achieving goals and delivering on customer expectations, every time. When someone underperforms, it's acknowledged and discussed. All those involved take what they can from the lesson and move on. It's critical to admit mistakes. If mistakes are overlooked, everyone will simply believe that the Destination is not that important. Mistakes do happen! We learn from them and then get back on track toward the Destination.

Many managers still try to get people to perform with the outdated punishment methods that end up in a Dilbert cartoon—threatening, embarrassing, or intimidating the employee into submission. These techniques do everything except provide a vehicle for getting things done. We encourage managers to provide a healthy pressure to perform through a focused, genuine, and interactive management approach.

We once facilitated a focus group at a leading hospital. The topic under discussion was how to become a great workplace, and a key issue on the table was performance expectations. As the discussion reached a boiling point, one of the participants slammed down her daytimer. She stood up and said, "I am a doctor here. Every single day, I save lives. I want you all to know I don't do it because I'm inspired by leadership. I do it in spite of them."

Translation? This doctor was feeling an unhealthy pressure to perform. What a different experience she would be having—and how different the patient experience would be—if hospital leadership applied a healthy pressure to perform!

>> *Do your people feel a sense of urgency to perform? What motivates them to do a good job, even when no one is watching?*

One Minute on the Treadmill

We've found that one of the best ways to apply healthy pressure is to take a "one minute on the treadmill" approach. If your goal is to run 35 minutes on a treadmill, you could look at it either as an entire 35-minute project or as a series of 1-minute projects. Imagine the difference in focus, motivation, or ability to simply do it! You'd celebrate at every interval. Not only would you be more focused; you'd be more attuned to what your body is telling you about the need to reserve fuel, add speed, or change the course.

Successful managers have learned the art of understanding the larger picture and also the value of being able to get something done in smaller parts. Make sure that after your managers paint the big picture for their people, they provide incremental steps for getting there and check in frequently as dictated by employees' ability to execute. We're not advocating that a manager look over the shoulder of every team member, but we are suggesting a close look at the contributions being amassed toward the Destination.

We usually get asked how often a manager needs to look into a project. The answer is that you have a range of options, depending on the project's urgency. For some projects, we've actually advocated an "every eight hours" managing philosophy, in which you check in on progress every day.

Sound controlling? Maybe. Yet sometimes we all need the extra structure and support provided by frequent checks on our progress. If you take this approach, however, let the person know why you'll be checking in so frequently. This approach is an excellent focus tool, and in times of crisis or when there's an extreme need to get something done, it can feel very supportive for the individuals doing the work. Instead of controlling people and looking over their shoulders, managing in eight-hour segments allows you to make sure every person is progressing toward the Destination.

The "every eight hours" philosophy can just as easily be adjusted for managing every day, week, or month, depending on the project and the goal for completion. The reason we advocate this interactive and focused management approach is that your people could readily reach the Destination if they were not responsible for so many other tasks. It's difficult for most employees to gauge what's really important in their organization. They'll take their cues from what their manager asks about. They'll want to know that the Destination is real and that their manager thinks it's real, too! At the same time, managers who take the "every eight hours" approach will know at all times what their people are experiencing so they can intervene as necessary and provide rewards—or correct the course.

We find that although most employees don't want a manager hovering over them, many are equally concerned about the manager who gives them little direction and has virtually no expectations. When people are new at a task, they need extra support, guidance, and direction. This feels supportive, not restrictive. As employees demonstrate their capabilities, the manager can support them by keeping more distance.

At times, you may need to get in the way of some employees. Cultural misfits are not only expensive; they're highly detrimental to Destination Planning. They intentionally or unintentionally sabotage other people and prevent them from doing their best work. Intervene with these employees immediately and prepare them for success—or prepare their exit strategy.

> > *Do you and your managers check in when your people are struggling? Can you tell who's disconnecting, who can't deliver his or her contribution regularly, and who's showing a change in behavior that signals something isn't right?*

Motivation through a Connected Culture

We believe leaders can't motivate people to reach a Destination. People motivate themselves. They're inspired by two things alone: the work itself and their connection to the larger organization or cause.

Sunny Vanderbeck, Data Return's CEO, suggests that a connected culture does more than spark people's minds. It involves their hearts.

"When thinking about culture, people, and business,
it's important to remember one overriding truth.
People don't care with their minds."
—Sunny Vanderbeck, CEO, Data Return

Job candidates at the Ritz-Carlton are screened to ensure that they have the caring attitude required to serve and the pride that comes from delivering superior service. The hotel chain's connected culture has shaped its accountability to service excellence. When you visit a Ritz-Carlton hotel, you find that it has carefully planned for your arrival in every way possible. If you need to get to another area of the hotel, a staff member will escort you there. When you stay at a Ritz-Carlton in Atlanta and request foam pillows, you can be sure that on your next visit to the Ritz-Carlton in Detroit, you'll find foam pillows in your room, thanks to a report that records your history with the hotel. The staff at the Ritz-Carltons are motivated to provide this level of service because they are part of a legacy of excellence in service. Their motto is "Ladies and gentlemen serving ladies and gentlemen." Accountability is ingrained in their culture. They don't need extra trinkets and coaching; it's just how they do business.

>> *Are people in your organization motivated through their connection to their jobs and to the greater good? Or do they look to their leaders to motivate them?*

If the right people are in the right jobs, motivation is an inherent part of the equation. Understand how people connect to their jobs or to the greater good, and use that as the motivation. Then, intentionally focus on helping people do what they like to do and what they do well—which is a great way to keep them connected with the business.

If people are doing what they like to do, doing it well, and feeling connected to the business, that's the ideal reward. People naturally like to do a good job, and when they can actually complete tasks that matter, the rewards are meaningful! A reward is usually welcome but not all are meaningful. Any reward you give an employee will always mean more when the basic reward is in the job or the connection to the business. You could give employees raises, recognition dinners, or even spot bonuses, but if you do that when they hate their jobs, you've simply wasted a great gift. Giving people recognition for doing something they love to do is a total win for everyone.

> *"Our performance evaluations are based on values-driven behavior—measuring how well our people uphold our cultural values of safety integrity, commitment, and excellence."*
> —Pat Jannausch, Vice President of Culture
> and Training, Con-way

This is not to discount recognition programs or other ways of showcasing people's achievements. We like those things, too, but don't believe they're enough to motivate your people. If more rewards are needed, reward through experiences—from on-the-spot praise, to a three-minute standing ovation at a group meeting, to a spontaneous gift of some time off. Set up a system that helps you reward people quickly, effectively, and often.

>> *How does your organization reward people?*

A Contribution-Oriented Culture

A contribution-oriented culture is one in which the focus has moved from performance to contribution. Instead of waiting until the end of the year to evaluate performance, gauge contribution in small steps. It's much more effective to praise employees for progress when they make it instead of waiting until the end of the year. Praise and coach frequently, and base feedback on employees' contributions to the organization.

Through one-on-one meetings, managers provide intentional feedback on reaching the Destination. It's not about the individual. It's about how the individual can accomplish things that contribute to reaching the Destination.

We're strong advocates of dismantling traditional performance reviews, as mentioned in chapter 5. This is a major step toward becoming a contribution-focused culture. Nearly every performance management system we've ever seen has more downsides than upsides. Here's how it usually goes:

1. HR sets up a schedule using forms that range from 1 to 10 pages in length.

2. HR puts the forms on the company intranet or gives them to managers to complete.

3. Managers usually wait until they have time to complete the forms—typically, late at night or on the weekend—and hope that the employee's self-evaluation will be substantial enough to fill in all the blanks HR has assigned.

4. The employee worries about the review, not so much because of the money, but because he or she hasn't received feedback all year long and doesn't know what to expect. Since people generally don't like to be rated, and when they are rated they want high marks only, they begin these meetings feeling anxious, just waiting for the bad news.

Even though the forms all say this is about the performance, not the person, no one really believes it.

The Contribution Coaching Model was developed by Modern-Think as a way of replacing traditional performance reviews.[1] Contribution Coaching is based on three foundations: the organization's Destination, the customer's needs, and the employee's needs. Reviews are conducted every 12 weeks and are designed to measure contributions toward the Destination, ability to deliver the customer experience, and the employee's ability to take care of himself or herself personally and professionally. It's a tool anyone can use with anyone else—supervisor to subordinate, subordinate to supervisor, and colleague to colleague.

> > *Are you gauging contribution in small steps, or relying on annual performance evaluations? Do your people know what is negotiable and what is nonnegotiable in your organization?*

Constructive Feedback

Have you ever attended a social function and, while speaking with another guest, noticed a piece of food stuck on her front tooth? Many of us don't say anything because we don't want to embarrass the person. The truth is that, in doing so, we've only spared them some embarrassment in the short term but certainly not in the long term. If the roles were reversed, we would rather know sooner than later, despite some initial awkwardness, so that we could correct the situation immediately.

In the same way, some managers fall into the trap of withholding feedback for fear of hurting an employee's feelings, but they run the risk of hurting that person's career instead. They need to give meaningful, contribution-focused, and frequent feedback.

Whenever your managers give someone corrective feedback, encourage them to follow these short and to-the-point guidelines:

- Tell employees what they're doing right 9 times out of 10, and tell them what you would like them to do differently 1 time out of 10.

- Refocus them on the steps you've outlined with them to get to the Destination.

- Keep feedback short, private, and immediate. If you wait more than a day to give it, the opportunity has passed.

Instant Coaching, or IC, is a concept we've developed that signals two key behaviors in managing: timely feedback and coaching. IC relies on a manager's ability to always be on the lookout for what's going right and what needs realignment. We like this method because it's quick and immediate, and it offers direction when the employee needs it. IC can be done daily and provides a consistent and healthy pressure to perform by keeping attention on contributions made toward reaching the Destination. When realignment is needed, it's usually because competing priorities interfered, something personal has affected an employee's ability to focus, or a person has lost momentum in going from one step to the next. Regardless of the reason, the manager's goal is to maximize contribution. The best way to do that is to keep the team focused on delivering on the Destination.

> > *Are your managers giving meaningful, contribution-focused, and frequent feedback?*

Meetings That Matter

In today's fast-paced world of information overload, everyone is buried in way too much stuff—too many e-mails, too many voice mails, and too many meetings! They're looking for ways to reduce the time spent on tasks that really don't add value. Infusing accountability throughout your organization requires that meetings be focused and used to accelerate, not confine, progress.

If you look at your calendar, chances are that most of the day is chock-full of internal meetings. Which of those meetings help you move toward your Destination? Which get in the way? Meet only when it will take you a step closer to your Destination or will produce some advancement for the organization.

When was the last time you had a really effective meeting? We've found that people who tend to schedule a lot of meetings usually have more capacity to execute and deliver but just aren't focused properly. Many people schedule meetings because it feels like they're getting something done. What they're really doing, though, is draining away precious resources as they're trying to make something happen. SC Johnson has outlawed meetings every other Friday so that employees can get some work done!

> **>> How can you eliminate meaningless meetings? What could you get done if you had half of the usual weekly meetings?**

Members of a leadership team asked us to help them evaluate the effectiveness of their meetings because everyone left with a different interpretation of discussions and decisions. We determined that leaders were trying to address too many issues in one meeting, and the details did not stay with attendees after they left the room.

We recommended implementing a daily 30-minute check-in meeting, a weekly contributions meeting, and a quarterly Destination Attainment meeting. By making this adjustment, they could all stay focused on the Destination and be much clearer on the steps needed to reach it. They could also be more productive because their energy and commitment were higher, and they would be spending much less time in wasted meetings.

Hold meetings only when you have the clearest Destination for each meeting, including what is to be discussed, what is to be decided, and who is to take the lead in doing which task.

>> *How many company hours per year are spent in meetings? Now contrast that with the hours spent with external customers.*

What Every Manager Needs to Know

In order to maximize accountability, every manager should know four basic pieces of information about the people he or she supervises:

1. Who they are as persons
2. How they absorb new information and respond to change
3. What disconnects them from the organization
4. How to leverage their abilities and work around their limitations

It's difficult to hold people accountable if you don't understand how they work and, more important, how they work best.

Personal Profile

The more your managers know about each person they manage, the more they can effectively lead, coach, and support their people; the better off their teams will be; and the more they can leverage each person's talents to further the business.

Each manager should try to put people's skills to work in ways that may not be apparent on the job. A person who loves to cook no doubt has great project management skills. An administrative assistant with a penchant for writing may make a robust contribution to her group's communications. Knowing about employees' family situations is equally important. If a person might have time conflicts when children get sick, those needs could be a consideration in scheduling workflow.

Learning Style

We all learn and absorb information differently. Good managers understand the learning style of each person on their teams.

Visual learners pick up information from what they see or read. They're particularly sensitive to facial expressions and body language and learn best from visual displays such as diagrams and pictures.

Auditory learners learn by listening. They thrive on discussions, talking things through, and absorbing what others have to say. Written information may have little meaning until it's heard.

Kinesthetic learners learn by moving, touching, and experiencing. The hands-on approach is the best one for them, because it allows them to actively explore the physical world around them. They may find it hard to sit still for long periods and might become distracted by their need for activity and exploration.

We all learn using a combination of visual, auditory, and kinesthetic abilities, but, for most of us, one style dominates. People will learn and retain more if information is presented to them in the learning style they prefer.

Disconnects

Managers need to understand what makes people disconnect from the team and the organization. Most people disconnect when they offer ideas that are met with nay-saying, for example,

"That'll never work here" or "We've tried that before." It's an invitation to instant shutdown. Others disconnect when they can't get a word in because other people on the team talk too much. Some tune out when they feel they can't trust others or aren't trusted themselves. Managers need to spot these points of disconnect instantly and help people reconnect just as quickly.

A member of a senior leadership team tells the story of his disconnection. When the CEO was hiring a new VP of HR, the CEO told him that no one on the current HR team would be allowed to interview her. "That's all it took," he says. "I immediately disengaged from the entire hiring process and found it difficult to connect with her when she came on board."

People will not feel positive about something they're not involved in. They won't exactly be unsupportive; they'll be neutral. Like a car stuck in neutral, a team of neutral players goes nowhere.

Leveraging Abilities, Bypassing Limitations

Know what your people do well and help them get around what they don't do well. If your Destination requires extreme amounts of detail, and your managers know some team members are more comfortable in the big-picture world of strategy, they can immediately implement a plan to help these team members work around their limitations. You don't want to lose them; you want to use their strengths and bypass their liabilities.

At W. L. Gore, the company's Commitment Principle suggests that each associate needs to make his or her own commitments and then deliver on them. The company tries diligently to understand each person's strengths and how these strengths can be best supported. If an associate isn't living up to his or her potential, Gore first ensures that the right person is in the right role. If that doesn't work, according to CEO Terri Kelly, the company seeks an alternative. That may include separation from Gore. The best system of checks and balances, Kelly adds, is peer support.

"If a person can't make and keep his
or her commitments, it's the rest of the
team that has to pull the weight."
—Terri Kelly, CEO, W. L. Gore & Associates, Inc.

Alston & Bird uses coaching, internal and external, to help get people on board with its Destinations. Chief Human Resources Officer Cathy Benton tells the story of a new manager who, though she'd been through orientation, was having difficulty living the firm's values. The manager was coached to better understand A&B culture—and then given time to make the change. "We want people to succeed," Benton says. "When we see that they're not, because of their relationships with people—and relationships are so important here—we do everything we can to help them."

Constraints on the Destination

As you move through Accountability, consider constraints that may impede progress to your Destination—at the individual and the team level. We hope you identified any constraints as you assessed the organization's alignment, but we always encourage continued focus on identifying and removing constraints.

Pull your leadership team together. Put your Destination on the wall. Then brainstorm using Exercise 5 to see what connects each person and team to the business and to the Destination, and what gets in the way. We call this the Destination Analysis, our version of the traditional force field analysis. It's a diagnostic tool that helps you understand what you need for delivering on the Destination. You can use this tool at both individual and team levels to ensure that the Destination and the driving forces necessary to reach it are clear. Then, put together an action plan for weakening any constraints in the right-hand column. Realign

DESTINATION ANALYSIS

On a whiteboard or a piece of paper, draw a large T. Write your Destination at the top of the T. On the left-hand side of the T, list all the reasons why you want to reach this Destination. For example,

- More applicants
- Less turnover
- Enhanced productivity
- Better working conditions
- More fun

On the right-hand side of the T, list everything that could be a constraining force and will maintain the stagnant quo. For example,

What might keep us from reaching our Destination

- Lack of trust
- People not treated equally
- Competitors outshining us
- Sub-par benefits package
- Average raise last year of 2.5 percent

The tool works this way: You don't push on the left-hand column. Those forces are already pushing change to happen. But the things on the right are locking you in place. Prioritize the constraints you've listed according to which one, if removed, would most likely make change happen. Begin taking action that weakens the items on the right. The line in the middle of the T will start to get pushed over by those things on the left because they are already accelerating change. It's those things on the right that need to be weakened so that you can continue the acceleration.

priorities so that you're held accountable for reaching the Destination in a way that works for your team and for each team member.

>> *What constraints are standing in the way of your reaching the Destination? How can you weaken them?*

Accountable People = Adaptable People

The ultimate win of Accountability is adaptability. Accountable employees are nimbler in adapting to changing circumstances. It's a lot like what happens in a basketball game. Employees need to be able to react to emerging opportunities, just as basketball players react to a loose ball or a sudden open path to the basket. Team members who know they're accountable for responding— and are empowered to respond because it's built into their team culture—are better able to seize the opening, improvise, and score. Accountable employees do the same: they meet opportunity head-on with innovation and charge forward with confidence toward the team's Destination.

[7] ADAPTATION

Evolving Every Day

Now that you've been through the phases of Awareness, Alignment, and Accountability, you're close to arriving at the most profitable part of the 4-A Process: Adaptation. In this phase, the only thing you need to do is adapt to ongoing changes.

We wish it were as simple as it sounds! The fact is, the better you are at adapting, the more you can stay ahead of the changes needed to continuously accelerate business growth. While the first three phases of the process are necessary, the ideal is to move through them fairly rapidly so that you can spend the most time in Adaptation. If your aim is to be a great workplace, for example, once you arrive at that Destination, you simply adapt as necessary to maintain your place there instead of going back to Awareness. However, during a merger, you would need to take the new company back through the 4-A Process to ensure that the organization can operate in true Adaptation mode.

Today, we're constantly breaking barriers in the speed of global commerce. Can you remember a time not too long ago when a written response took a full week to reach you because it had to be mailed? And now, we can send an e-mail to the other side of the world and get the reply in just seconds.

> *"More and more, our customers and competitors*
> *are global. All the more reason for us to know*
> *exactly what we stand for. It gives us a thread of*
> *consistency in competing throughout the world."*
>
> —Anne Kenlon, Corporate Spokesperson, Corning Incorporated

Competing in meaningful ways today requires your organization to adapt as speed barriers are continuously broken. The fundamental question that shapes Adaptation is this: Can your organization adapt faster than the world around you is changing? Before you answer, remember that Albert Einstein defined insanity as doing the same things over and over—each time expecting a different result!

Adaptation is more than an activity. It's a mind-set. Every strategy used in this phase must also be aligned with the needs of your customers, and this can be a challenge, given that customers' needs evolve. Organizations must stay focused on measuring the results of contributions, as it's not possible to measure adaptability as a skill. We must stay focused on measuring those business metrics that ultimately meet the demands of our employees, customers, and partners.

Adaptation is not a management fad. It's a proven way to compete. With every team and every individual externally informed and internally driven, your organization can predict and plan for change. With an Adaptation mind-set, you won't need 3-, 5-, and 10-year plans. You'll be able to see the indicators of change long before you're forced to change—adapting with seamless agility to outpace your competitors in any economy and pursuing any Destination.

An Endless Cycle

Creating successful and profitable organizations is a goal that's never completed. It's an endless cycle. Why? Because, just when your organization reaches its Destination, me-too companies jump into the game. It's not a question of *will* you have more competition but *when* will you—and how difficult will it be for your competitors to do what you do for the same, or less, cost.

You, like others, need loyal customers who believe you understand their needs and will deliver on them time after time. From a benchmark perspective, you need to be able to compete with the world's best in whatever you're doing, because today's customers have an endless array of choices, and space for new business is getting pretty tight!

Fresh ways of creating value must not be left with start-up companies that pride themselves on their speed and agility. With the technological advancements and globalization that characterize today's marketplace, innovation is an imperative for every company. Those that haven't learned to adapt are in a precarious position. Not only are U.S. businesses competing with one another; they're competing with products and services from around the world and with a constant influx of new ideas and talent. Competition is also coming from different industries. Many children today would be more thrilled to get a Sony PlayStation than they would be about going to the circus. Did Barnum & Bailey ever plan to compete with Sony?

Airlines like Southwest and JetBlue made it cheaper to fly to some places than to drive. And both these airlines forged into markets that had enhanced capacity instead of trying to take business from already-established legacy carriers. This happened anyway, but it wasn't their leading strategy. Both JetBlue and Southwest understood that the flying public was ready for airlines to adapt and built an entirely new way of doing business.

Adaptation versus Change Management

With all of the mergers, restructuring, and downsizing that have taken place over the past few decades, consulting gurus cooked up the concept of "change management." Basically, you have a company that has done the same thing for a really long time until it's well overdue for some updating and then turn the entire organization upside down: drastically alter jobs, lay people off, tilt the direction of the company 180 degrees. Afterward, help everyone deal with the trauma of the change, a process that can last one to two years and beyond. The company was already several years behind its competition when it realized it needed to make some serious changes. And now it will take another few years to recover from those changes. At which point, it may be time to change everything all over again.

Adaptation is about making small adjustments along the way. It's about constantly monitoring progress, building on what's working, and fine-tuning what needs improvement—and always staying one step ahead of the competition. This is a much healthier, less traumatic, approach to keeping your organization on the cutting edge.

Purpose beyond Profit

Perhaps no event has been a greater test of adaptability than the 9/11 national disaster. As organizations dealt with the ramifications of 9/11, we found many amazing stories of people who went above and beyond to help one another. We also found that the stronger the organization, meaning the more connected people were to the organization, the better it dealt with the tragedy that forever changed our world.

Founded as an organization that cares, JetBlue Airways fully demonstrated just how much it cares in the first moments of 9/11. As the air traffic system shut down at John F. Kennedy International Airport in New York, JetBlue crew members went to work immediately. Several neighboring airlines rolled down the covers of their service desks and officially closed, perhaps because they were not prepared to deal with the situation in any other way. JetBlue took in these airlines' customers as its own. JetBlue leaders secured the largest ballroom at a hotel across the street from JFK. They had 500 beds brought in and fed and housed people for three days, regardless of what airline the travelers were ticketed with. Shuttle vans went on diaper and medicine runs, and the airline even brought in entertainment to help ease the pain and uncertainty people were experiencing. When asked why they chose to do this, JetBlue leadership responded simply, "We are JetBlue."

In the late 1990s, when airline analysts and competitors first talked about JetBlue, the company was often compared with People Express. JetBlue likes being compared with its predecessor because People was a "paradigm breaker," Mike Barger says. The reaction to JetBlue's arrival was similar to the reaction to People's arrival in 1981: "It'll never fly."

When People Express was founded, it was set to revolutionize the airline industry. For several years, this start-up phenomenon took off by charging customers for everything from in-flight snacks to checked luggage. By January 1986, People Express had grown to be the fifth-largest airline in the United States and had revenues of about $1 billion per year. Its innovative management style and structure were praised as the wave of the future, and companies around the world rushed to imitate its innovations. Yet, by September 1986, People was bankrupt and ended up being acquired by Continental Airlines. What went wrong? People Express became misaligned when it deviated from its Optimum People-Profit Opportunity by purchasing long-range aircraft for overseas travel, and, by the time it realized this, it couldn't adapt quickly enough to get back on track.

JetBlue, however, took off and continues to soar. Unlike People, it hasn't lost sight of its business plan and doesn't charge anything for its delicious blue chips and 36 channels of satellite TV! While People got bogged down in trying to be something it wasn't, JetBlue is busy being everything it is, poised to adapt to any situation it faces.

Considering that the airline industry has lost more money in the past 5 years than it has made in the past 50 years, tremendous lessons can be learned from observing other airlines' shortfalls. And if we've learned anything about JetBlue Airways, we know it will make very good use of these lessons.

> > *How will you grow your business and stay focused on what you do best? How will you help your organization leverage your OPPOs?*

Everyone Can Do It

As human beings, we're remarkably adaptable, able to bend and blend with an always evolving environment. It's the same with the organizations we create: Every organization has the ability to adapt, regardless of size, industry, and life cycle.

Adaptation happens in a variety of ways, from adjusting the internal culture to enhancing the customer experience. The pathway to Adaptation is different in every organization, because every organization has a unique set of characteristics, which respond differently to external conditions. These characteristics must be folded into helping the organization develop the capacity to adapt. Remember, you need to know what you're really good at so you can leverage your strengths for future adaptations.

The goal of the Adaptation phase is to understand what external changes will affect your organization internally so that you can routinely make small adjustments rather than have to implement massive cultural change. This isn't to say that you won't need some significant change in the beginning. You might indeed. Once your organization reaches a Destination, though, it should plan to operate at that high level of productivity and make tweaks as it continues to grow.

>> *What unique characteristics of your organization can best help you adapt?*

SAS Institute has been ahead of the adaptation curve since its days as a start-up. It launched its daycare center in 1981, responding to the needs of a new mother who was struggling with the decision of whether to come back to work or stay at home with her child. "We knew we could help her with her dilemma, so we started a daycare center," says Jeff Chambers, vice president of human resources. This amenity not only met an employee need but became a distinct benefit that helped the company retain employees.

Southwest Airlines continuously demonstrates its ability to be nimble in the face of any threat. When the company launched a new advertising campaign, it discovered that its slogan, "Just plane smart," was already owned by a small aviation company, South Carolina–based Stevens Aviation. Rather than spending several years and several hundred thousand dollars in litigation, Southwest and Stevens agreed to an arm-wrestling match at the Sportatorium Arena in Dallas.

Herb Kelleher, Southwest's chairman at the time, took on Stevens chairman Kurt Herwald, the prize being the rights to the coveted slogan. The goal was to arm wrestle it out, give some money to charity to legitimize the event, and garner as much publicity as possible in the process. The 61-year-old Kelleher was showcased as "Smokin' Herb," on a training diet of cigarettes and Wild Turkey; 38-year-old Herwald turned out to be a bodybuilder!

On the day of the match, the stands filled with hundreds of cheering teams from Southwest and Stevens. Once in the ring, Smokin' Herb, dressed in a T-shirt, sweat pants, and boxing trunks, retired to an easy chair in one corner. In the other corner, his opponent sat on a three-legged stool adorned with fake sticks of dynamite.

Herwald dispatched the much older Smokin' Herb in seconds. To the surprise and delight of the audience, the companies announced that they would both continue to use the "Just plane smart" slogan after all. Conclusion? The whole event was a brilliant publicity ploy—confirmed by Kelleher's last words as he was wheeled out of the arena on a stretcher to face the paparazzi. "I don't care what you say about me," he said. "Just remember my name."

By adapting to the situation, Southwest turned a marketing effort that could have been very costly into a marketing effort that was far more successful than the original.

> > *Is your organization better at doing things the same way, or does it excel at trying new ways of doing things?*

From Fragmentation to Focus

As we discussed in chapter 4, even among those companies that have kept up technologically, most are still operating with a two-centuries-old division-of-labor mentality. Each person focuses on doing his or her small part of a larger task that collectively produces something for the customer. That's often an invitation to fragmentation and breakdown. It's also a concern, as change happens best when organizations are focused on a few, but very important, Destinations. The more fragmented the organization, the slower the pace of change.

> >> *Does your organization follow the division-of-labor model, or can you adapt readily to environmental changes? Is your structure designed to compete or just to get by?*

Many management theories have tried to revamp the old model with approaches such as Total Quality Management, One-Minute Management, reengineering, downsizing, rightsizing, Quality Circles, Six Sigma—you name it. But these solutions produce limited results. That's because they're based on fixing one action or variable instead of teaching the entire organization to adapt to any circumstance.

Why did newcomer Newcor Steel thrive, while once-dominant Bethlehem Steel became extinct? It was the strong insistence of Bethlehem's leadership that they knew best when dealing with the steel industry and their failure to make the internal changes needed to compete. Unlike many legacy companies, start-ups are free of outdated belief systems and can readily adapt to environmental changes. In fact, start-ups are often launched by people tired of the old way of doing things. A legacy mentality is not a viable plan for future growth, as newcomers to your industry can simply outmaneuver your organization.

The goal of any legacy organization today must be to redefine and reinvent how it does business in today's environment, creating new market space instead of trying to take someone else's. If you rely only on past success to give you the information you need to survive in the future, remember that everyone has access to that information. Instead, ask yourself what you see that they don't. That's where you'll find your unique market position and certainly your Optimum People-Profit Opportunity.

> > *What ideas in your organization that fail to get implemented could result in profit explosions for your company? How equipped is your workforce for both imposed and planned change?*

An Integrated Customer Experience

Organizations need to bring their business and thinking models up to speed with today's customer expectations, and customer expectations have never been higher! Why? Because the competition has taught them to expect more. Flying on an airplane can be fun and entertaining, coffee can be prepared a thousand different ways, and packages can be sent across the county in less than 24 hours. Customers have a plethora of choices about where to spend their money, and they have valuable information you need to grow your business.

No one wants to be bounced around to multiple people or departments for answers. Customers want one point of contact that will get them everything they need. But how often does this happen? Instead, we hear variations on "That's not my job. Let me transfer you to someone else who can help you."

An organization that can provide an integrated customer experience is well positioned to outperform the competition and find new ways of strengthening its customers' experience so that they will continue to turn to that company to fulfill their needs.

It's an out-of-the-silo approach that focuses less on tasks and more on the collective ability to deliver on customer demands.

Whirlpool has carved out an individualized approach to customer service. When customers call the company, they're typically routed to the servicepeople who helped them the last time they called. That kind of creative thinking is a hallmark of the Adaptation phase. Imagine calling Whirlpool, and the serviceperson says, "Oh yes, I spoke to you last month. How's the new dishwasher?" It's an instant connection—and a much better chance to provide an excellent customer experience.

JetBlue has helped its crew members adapt to whatever is happening with its customers—and turn the customer experience around, if needed. According to Mike Barger, "It's pretty cool when you can take some of those folks who've had a long travel day and turn them around so that they walk away from the ticket counter and the JetBlue experience with a smile on their faces—completely stunned by the incredible service they just received."

> *"Having a stake in everyone's goals ensures that we hit our strategic objectives across the organization."*
> —Susan Johnston, HR Director, East Alabama Medical Center

East Alabama Medical Center has had the same core values for 20 years but continuously adapts to meet the needs of its four constituent groups: patients, physicians, community, and employees. Strategic planning involves cross-functional teams so that "everyone understands what's going on in all departments," says HR Director Susan Johnston.

> >> *How is your organization finding new ways to delight your customers? What recovery plan do you use when customers' expectations are not met?*

Change Reactions

If we want to understand how people respond to change, it's important to realize that forced or imposed change triggers a clear and fairly predictable pattern in most of us. Just think about what happens daily at airports around the world. The minute a flight is canceled, it triggers a series of emotional reactions in the crowd—frustration, stress, anger. These reactions happen when change is forced on us and we lose our ability to influence the outcome.

Imagine if the captain of the plane met with the passengers and explained about the bad weather and the faulty valve in the engine, and they decided together to cancel the flight. The reaction would probably be very different.

We've found that when relationships are healthy, when employees are connected to your business and have been included in planning, strategizing, and executing changes, emotional reactions are significantly minimized.

If your organization must adapt quickly to a situation and there's simply not time to confer with employees, be ready for their reactions, acknowledge them, and get on with adapting. It would be ideal if your people could respond with enthusiasm and vigor to every adaptation, but, in reality, they probably won't. However, being aware of typical reactions to change and knowing how to help people through them are parts of a useful strategy.

The following are typical responses to forced or imposed change:

- **Shock, surprise.** This is the initial reaction to forced or unplanned change. Depending on the current state of preparedness, this reaction may range from a barely noticeable gesture to a highly emotional outpouring. People are reacting to the possibility of a threat to the status quo, which is always disturbing.

How to handle: Listen, listen, listen. Telling people to calm down when they are experiencing these emotions adds more anxiety and stress. They need to process their emotional reactions, through being listened to, and their tactical reactions, by figuring out alternative courses of action.

- **Rejection, denial of current information.** The next reaction typically is rejection or denial. As a way of coping, people just try to block out the change. Sometimes this actually works! Other times, an alternative is found and the change isn't implemented. Or people may withhold their support or participation to such an extent that the proposed change becomes difficult or impossible to implement.

How to handle: Again, listen, and help people work through their reactions. Make sure that they keep their assessment real and refrain from exaggerating the situation. This is difficult, but necessary, to keep them moving through their emotional reaction to imposed change.

- **Blame, self-blame.** When the reality of the imposed change does sink in, employees may feel the need to blame others or themselves. Some employees may express a variety of negative reactions or direct challenges. The most even-tempered people may experience slight flare-ups as they work through inconveniences brought by the change.

How to handle: Listen and coach, so people fully understand that, regardless of who's responsible for the change, they can find a way to make the new situation work for them.

- **Problem-solving.** This is the time to consider the new options. Now, there is a steady progression from incompetence to competence, from being out of control to getting back some control. Depending on the ease and success of the transition, employees' reactions to the change can be very positive and rewarding.

How to handle: Keep listening and help people brainstorm options for the next steps. Be a facilitator, as opposed to a solver, which will enable them to explore choices and ultimately choose and adapt to their new paths.

The Signals

The more hierarchical organizations become, the less likely they are to see what's going on all around them. When Ford Motors announced "Quality is Job 1," it was a long way behind competitors who had been making quality a priority for years. Overseas automakers like Toyota and Honda had a much better understanding of what customers were willing to pay more for and were also aware that consumers had made a connection between quality and safety. At one time, the name Ford became an acronym for a phrase that signaled anything but quality: Found On Road Dead.

The 4-A Process would have been an excellent one for Ford to use to roll out this new Destination. When Ford's quality campaign was first launched, it followed the usual model: An edict from corporate leadership without any real employee support. Ford leaders thought it was an excellent Destination—and it was—but employees didn't believe the new slogan was anything more than marketing spin. When behaviors inside Ford didn't change and quality declined dramatically, leaders realized they needed to make fundamental changes in internal operations. This was the perfect time for Awareness to be spread throughout the organization.

>> *How do your employees know that you're serious about your Destination?*

When Ford employees eventually saw that leadership was serious about quality, behavior shifted and better cars were made. Now, quality at Ford is a built-in part of how they do business, and the company simply adapts to new changes as new markets are created.

Ford's latest version of the Mustang—the popular model that first rolled off the assembly line in Dearborn, Michigan, in 1964—commands a 10-month wait for would-be purchasers. Talk about Adaptation!

How do companies realize the need to adapt? Every organization needs to be so close to its customers that it can see signals of change and predict the changes it must make. This form of Adaptation delivers customers' needs before they even know they have the needs. Did anyone really need to ship something overnight before FedEx? How about cell phones and pagers, boomboxes and iPods? Yes, people did manage before cell phones and iPods. But you wouldn't know this today. Often, the best Adaptation results from creating a need for something that people did not know they needed before you offered it.

> *"We're constantly thinking at every level of our organization about what might be coming down the pike."*
>
> —Cathy Benton, Chief Human Resources Officer, Alston & Bird

> **>> What Destinations have been major successes for your organization? What was the most valuable output for your employees, partners, and customers?**

Intensive Listening

A key part of the Adaptation phase is getting feedback from all interested partners in your organization: employees, investors, the press, industry experts, consultants, and, of course, your customers. Without it, you're flying without radar!

Don't just assume that you know what your stakeholders need. Open up channels so they can give you insights into your business and help you discover new markets. In short, ask them, and then listen. Listen even when they don't speak. You need to know what your stakeholders think, how they think, and when they think about you.

> **>> How do you collect and process feedback from your stakeholders? How often?**

Weigh the relative importance of all options according to the best Destination for your organization. Most companies rely on qualitative data from industry experts. But what about the reactions from your partners? Do you know it, do you gather it, and does it guide you?

JetBlue is diligent about collecting feedback on the JetBlue experience from its stakeholders: 30 million customers, 11,000 crew members, and lots of interested investors. The company realizes it's not just selling a flight; it's selling an experience.

JetBlue responded rapidly to crew member feedback by setting up home reservation centers—becoming the first airline to accommodate the high demand to work out of the home. If you call JetBlue to make a reservation, there's a slight chance you'll connect to a reservations call center, but most likely you won't. "You're probably speaking to someone in jammies and fuzzy slippers," Mike Barger says. "The only time you'll get them at the reservation center is during their first two weeks on the job, when they're being trained to provide the JetBlue experience for you." Each reservation crew member is equipped with a secure phone and computer system, which enables them to help you safely and securely anytime.

We might think that most of the comments an airline receives are about the actual flight experience. But, even though JetBlue customers enjoy the company's many in-flight amenities, most of the feedback they offer is about JetBlue crew members and the experience they provide customers. This is an important piece of information for JetBlue. Any Adaptation must factor in this part of the equation so that the company can continue to provide the flying public with what people are really paying for: the JetBlue experience.

>> *How is information infused into every part of your business? When was the last time you had customers visit your organization and give you feedback on issues important to your business?*

Words That Work

Choosing language intentionally is a critical part of connecting people to the business and delivering the customer experience. As times have changed, companies have adapted their internal vocabularies to match.

For example, JetBlue calls all employees "crew members"— from customer service to in-flight personnel, from technical operations to JetBlue University staff.

We asked Mike Barger if "employees" is a bad word at JetBlue. He responded that the company uses it just once, and that's during orientation. "Traditionally, employees are called 'employees' in the airline industry. And that simply won't do for JetBlue," he says. "Just like we don't have a 'they' here. It's always 'we.'"

When you ask the people at JetBlue how many passengers they carry, they'll tell you zero. They don't view those who fly JetBlue as passengers—as something you haul around. They see them as customers—people they serve and take care of.

During our visit, we also asked about the company headquarters. We were politely but firmly informed that JetBlue has no headquarters. It does, however, have a support center, intended to bolster every crew member in the JetBlue organization and to take care of their every need, just as they serve others.

Wal-Mart calls its employees "associates," and it encourages managers to think of themselves as servant leaders. It calls employees at the front door—who welcome people into the store but also prevent shoplifting—"people greeters." It's Wal-Mart's way of helping you feel a little less like a number in a very large store!

At W. L. Gore & Associates, there are some words you will never hear—like "allowed to," "should have," and "because I'm the boss, that's why." It's an action-oriented language culture; in other words, "How do we get it done?"

Everyone at Gore is an "associate," because leaders believe that hierarchy limits innovation. Terri Kelly uses the title CEO in the outside world when needed; however, inside Gore she is one of 7,000 associates.

When someone at Gore quits or is fired, the company refers to it as a separation. This word acknowledges that a mind and a heart are leaving the organization, and it speaks to the relationship side of the separation instead of only to the procedure.

Performance reviews at Gore are known as contribution reviews. Gore believes less in evaluating performance, which is often based on politics, and more on the actual contributions the individual is making to the organization. There are no bosses, only leaders, who are responsible for getting the product out the door, and sponsors, who have influence. Their only goal is to ensure maximum contribution.

Having a language that works inside your organization enables Adaptation because the words have more meaning when they're unique to a culture or an organization. It's like having a secret code. By knowing the code, you feel a part of something.

All organizations can have their own language by simply deciding to do so. Language is extremely powerful and may be integrated into any culture. Just a few years ago, when you said you were going to "google" something on the Internet, no one would have known what you meant. Today, everything—and everyone—is getting googled!

>> *Does your organization's vocabulary enhance your people's connection to the business? What specific words can activate your organization?*

Externally Informed, Internally Driven

External threats and opportunities exist for all businesses. Recessions, mergers and acquisitions, natural disasters, bull markets, wars—they've always been with us. If all businesses face these conditions, yet some work through them seamlessly while others are disrupted, we have to conclude that it's what goes on internally— in response to external conditions—that makes or breaks a business.

Every industry goes through periods of growth and decline. Similarly, all companies—even the world's greatest workplaces— face ups and downs. No one is free from the turmoil of business, but no one is limited by it, either.

Regardless of external conditions, businesses must remain true to their functions of being able to deliver products or services to their customers and doing it in a way that creates a connection. If they succeed in doing that, it's because their people are aligned and can execute on their Destinations. They need to avoid the trap of blaming external markets and conditions if they fail, since these factors are beyond their control. Instead, organizations should be able to look within their own walls and see what's not connected or aligned with the external world.

We advocate an externally informed, internally driven approach—one in which companies constantly understand external conditions, build internal conditions into their organizations to address them, and anticipate and make changes as needed.

>> *What major forces have forced your organization to change in the past 18 months? What forces have constrained your organization from reaching its Destinations?*

An Eye on the Radar

What trends alerted Southwest to hedge fuel when its competitors didn't? And how about Wal-Mart, which figured out that whenever big storms are in the forecast, consumers tend to stock up on strawberry Pop-Tarts? This enables them to ship extra Pop-Tarts to stores that might be in the storm's path so that you, the consumer, have plenty of comfort food during the bad weather.

Business has no access to a magic fortune-teller; but those who consistently follow the trends have a better handle on change. Organizations that have mastered the art of Adaptation constantly monitor what's happening around them—competitors, customers, market and regulatory trends—as well as their internal culture and conditions. They see the signals and adapt their processes long before change sweeps through.

Like good pilots, adaptable leaders continuously gather information that will make their businesses more successful. They check the many gauges that monitor progress. They listen to what their copilots tell them and adjust the flight as needed, navigating the organization out of troubled areas and keeping it always en route to the Destination.

>> *In what ways are you developing relationships with your customers? With your competitors' customers?*

When Con-way was established in 1983, it faced a host of competitors, says Pat Jannausch, vice president of culture and training. The company made a deliberate effort to create an image that was more professional than those of its competitors and to encourage its drivers to build relationships. "Our drivers are called 'driver sales representatives.' They wear uniforms, carry business cards, and are trained to interact with the customers like salespeople, equipped to explain the key features and benefits of our company," she says. Another goal was to provide consistent service, creating a standard of 98 percent on-time performance for next-day and second-day deliveries. High standards for customer interaction enabled the company to set a premium price for its service.

Over the years, Con-way has fine-tuned its adaptability by being a flat organization and by pursuing its goal of maintaining high productivity while carefully managing both the cost structure and the culture.

>> *What are your competitors' five biggest worries? Do your competitors know what keeps you awake at night?*

Take What's Working and Do More of It

Did you ever get a report card with all As . . . and one C? Where did your attention go? On how to fix the C, right? Adaptable organizations focus on the As. They concentrate on what they do well rather than trying to fix everything. We wonder how different the learning process would be if teachers marked only the correct answers on tests—imagine 18 answers out of 20 being highlighted as "right."

As you know by now, we're not fans of traditional performance reviews. Employees are usually asked to complete development plans, which often commits them to doing something differently. We believe a more effective approach is to focus on the five or so things each employee does really well, instead of trying to fix what's perceived to be wrong. Leverage what's right in your employees! The real win is when you give people the opportunity to do more of what they're doing well.

This emphasis also works on the organizational level, especially when you're looking for new business growth. For example, instead of looking for long-haul flights, Southwest recognized its gift for short-haul flights and got even better at what it already was really good at doing! FedEx expanded its service from shipping letters overnight to speed shipping virtually any item, from furniture to freight trucks. We believe organizations that can expand market space while still leveraging their OPPOs can truly capitalize on the experience of their people.

Some companies have tried to expand their products or services into markets that, while connected to their business, were disconnected from their customers' vision of the company. At one time, Ben-Gay came out with aspirin. Sure, it was great from a technical perspective, but the public couldn't get past the thought that the tell-tale smell of Ben-Gay would somehow end up in the aspirin. Smuckers rolled out its own line of ketchup. It certainly made sense, since the company could make ketchup with technology similar to what it used to make its delicious jellies and jams. The problem was that no one wanted sweet-tasting ketchup, and sweetness is the quality most associated with Smuckers products.

> > *List the top reasons why your company is successful. Describe how each reason might enable more opportunities to sell your products and services.*

Strength from Employees' Knowledge and Needs

Your employees' ability to give you the information you need for your decision-making is critical. They'll be best poised to do that if you help them become experts in your business. Just as senior leaders may be more aware of market conditions, rank-and-file employees typically are more aware of what's going on inside the organization. Employees who also understand the external environment are better at making recommendations, feeding information to leadership, influencing decisions, and helping the organization adapt.

>> *How are you drawing on your employees' knowledge and needs?*

JetBlue realized it needed to minimize turnaround time on its aircraft. One of the most significant delays occurred when the ground crew tried to figure out the plane's weight. (And at an average cost of $100,000 per hour for a plane to be on the ground, time is of the essence!) JetBlue responded by giving its pilots laptop computers so that they could calculate weight, balance, and takeoff performance before actually taking off. It was the first airline to do so. Laptops also enable pilots to access electronic-format manuals during flight through a special application called—what else?—"Bluebooks."

JetBlue's laptops have also delivered better customer service. Pilots can go to the boarding gates and bring up real-time maps and weather updates and pass this information along to customers. JetBlue's founders realized that having laptops in the cockpits of planes would enhance flight safety because information could be immediately updated. JetBlue pilots can adapt very quickly to any situation and may be better able to stay on schedule when changes might affect the timing of a flight.

>> *What does your organization do that enables your employees to deliver the ideal customer experience? What revolutionary ideas might enable your people to better serve your customers?*

Kmart, Wal-Mart, and Target:
Three Stories of Adaptation

When we think of 1962, many of us remember it as the year John Glenn orbited the Earth three times. But, back on Earth, there was another series of three, this time in the world of retail. Sam Walton opened a 16,000-square-foot discount store called Wal-Mart. The Dayton Hudson Corporation launched a new retailing experience called Target. And the Canadian-based S. S. Kresge Company opened its first Kmart in Garden City, Michigan.

Today, Wal-Mart's sales have reached $286 billion annually, Target is at $46 billion, and Kmart comes in at a comparatively low $19 billion. Wal-Mart turns over each store's inventory about eight times a year, Target about seven times, and Kmart just over three and a half times. Given the same economic conditions, the same basic products being sold, and two with a previous retail history, why do we see dramatically different business results?

Our 4-A Process holds at least part of the answer. Wal-Mart and Target stayed focused on their OPPOs and never lost their ability to adapt to the changing needs of shoppers. Wal-Mart became an efficiency guru, ensuring a full supply of hundreds of thousands of products customers could purchase at "always low prices." Target adapted to trends by offering something for everyone who was interested in the latest fashions or home accessories. Kmart, in the first few years after 1962, was the biggest retailer compared to the other two. But it deviated from its original brand of discount retailing, became misaligned with its customers and employees, and couldn't keep up with the changing demands of the discount shopper.

Kmart—Destination: Moving Merchandise Quickly

Kmart's start was promising enough. In 1962, it opened 17 stores in addition to its founding store in Garden City. By 1966, it had just over 900 stores and $1 billion in sales—hitting the $1-billion milestone a full 13 years before Wal-Mart did. By 1981, it boasted more than 2,000 stores and had expanded outside the United States into Canada and Puerto Rico.

Throughout the 1980s and into the 1990s, Kmart bulked up, and added costs by acquiring retailers such as Borders and Sports Authority. Wal-Mart and Target, meanwhile, were keeping their focus: stocking their shelves with contemporary merchandise, staying in close touch with the needs of discount shoppers, and finding ways of reducing costs.

Kmart's missteps continued. Unlike Wal-Mart, the company did not invest in computer technology to manage its supply chain. It maintained a high dividend, reducing the resources available to improve its stores. Despite bringing in such upscale line names as Martha Stewart, Kathy Ireland, Jaclyn Smith, Disney, and Sesame Street, it was unable to create a consistent brand image.

What really happened to Kmart? Were Wal-Mart and Target to blame? Kmart was at one time best known for its widely popular Blue Light Special, started in the 1960s as a quick way to move clearance merchandise out of the store. At surprise moments, a store worker would light up a mobile blue police light, announcing a discount offer in different parts of the store. The phrase "Attention, Kmart shoppers" took a front seat in pop culture vocabulary, at one time registering an 80 percent familiarity rating with American consumers. But, by 1991, the Blue Light Special had disappeared, due in part, the company says, to changing consumer habits and misuse by individual stores.

In 2001, Kmart made an ill-fated attempted to reintroduce the Blue Light Special with its Blue Light Always marketing campaign, aimed to compete head-to-head with Wal-Mart's low prices. The plan went something like this: The Kmart store manager announces a 25-minute promotion in-store every hour, on the hour. When the special is announced over the loudspeaker, music fills the store, and all employees stop what they're doing, clap twice, and pump their fists in the air, shouting, "Blue Light, Blue Light!" The plan failed because stores didn't follow it. No one shouted "Blue Light, Blue Light!"

Why didn't employees follow the plan? We believe it's because they didn't have any idea of a clear Destination or connection to the business and therefore were not inclined to align with it or be held accountable for doing it. In short, Kmart culture didn't support such an outward expression of motivation, commitment, and passion. The company continues to hold on to flickers of its past success by reintroducing the Blue Light Special online. But is it too late?

Considering that many of Kmart's wares are the same as those offered by other retailers, somewhere along the way, shopping at Kmart became less appealing, and customers drove right past Kmart to Wal-Mart or Target. Bottom line? Kmart simply didn't adapt with the times. It became misaligned with its loyal discounting customers, and the misalignment stressed the organization. In contrast to its rivals, Kmart never seemed to settle on a clear Destination. In the end, more customers concluded that it was a better deal to shop at Wal-Mart and more in vogue to stop by Target.

With its recent acquisition of Sears, Kmart appears to be attempting to reinsert itself into the game and compete more robustly with Wal-Mart and Target. By sticking to what it knows best—discount retailing—Kmart can maintain a stronger focus and gain efficiencies in the overall organization. This could be an extraordinary turnaround for a company many had written off long ago. Will we again see the blue lights flashing? We hope so.

Wal-Mart—Destination: Aggressive Discounting

Since 1962, Wal-Mart has stayed close to Sam Walton's original Destination: bring value to customers through aggressive discounting and empower associates to make decisions. To align his operations with the Destination, Walton thought strategically about store locations. He flew his own small plane over much of Middle America, searching for lots that were large enough to host a Wal-Mart.

Wal-Mart has been particularly successful in aligning its buying practices. Its purchase of massive quantities of items from its suppliers, combined with a highly efficient stock control system, has helped keep operating costs lower than those of its competitors. The company's vast purchasing power gives it the leverage to force manufacturers to change their production, usually by creating cheaper products, to suit its wishes. A single Wal-Mart order may represent a double-digit percentage of a supplier's yearly output.

With more than 1.6 million employees, Wal-Mart has an enormous responsibility in just communicating with its staff. Yet, despite the amazing size of its workforce, it has managed to build a feeling of family in each of its stores, and this improves employees' ability to focus and hold themselves accountable to Wal-Mart's ultimate Destination: low prices. All employees are trained in the art of retailing and understand that their job is to push merchandise out the door. If Wal-Mart were to keep growing at the same rate for the next 20 years, it would employ nearly half of the world's population.

Leaders at Wal-Mart can hold their people accountable because Sam Walton designed this ability into the organization's culture. Everyone inside the organization knows that, at the end of the day, what is most critical for Wal-Mart is that it has sold as much merchandise as possible at the absolute lowest price. It's a Destination that seems to be crystal clear to everyone.

From the start, Wal-Mart has kept its eye on the radar screen, acutely aware of emerging trends and encroaching competitors. In the 1960s and 1970s, the company built its own infrastructure and distribution network. In the early 1980s, it was one of the first retailers to leverage bar codes to increase efficiency at checkout counters and provide real-time, point-of-sale information to manufacturers so it could gauge demand and eliminate the need for warehousing. This in turn led the company to develop Retail Link, its own trend-forecasting software for tracking consumer behavior. This revolutionary system delivered sophisticated information drawn from the data embedded in the bar codes. Wal-Mart shared its software with suppliers at no cost, to help them meet the retailer's needs more efficiently.

Wal-Mart today is the largest retailer, the largest company in the world based on revenue, and the largest private employer in Canada, Mexico, and the United States. *Forbes* points out that if Wal-Mart were its own economy, it would rank 23rd in the world, with a GDP between those of Austria and Saudi Arabia.

Target—Destination: Style

Target set its Destination, too, from the very beginning: to sell quality, stylish products at affordable prices while creating a fashionable image that would attract people who otherwise wouldn't be caught dead shopping in a discount store.

Target's branding strategy has changed little since its inception in 1962. It's clear about who it is as a company and has successfully implanted this image in the minds of its customers, aligning its advertising, marketing, and merchandise to provide a consistent customer experience. Stores are clean, spacious, and attractive, and merchandise is readily available. Consumers describe Target's merchandise as "trendy, but not trashy," unlike that found at the usual discount store.

When you go into a Target, you get the immediate sensation that something there is just a little groovier than your average store. The brightly colored shopping carts glide from wide aisle to wide aisle so you can load up on the latest hip products. How do you know it's hip? Because Target sells it. What a great way to align an organization, connect to the customer, and provide an automatic way of holding people accountable—through the experience that customers come there to get! Leaders of Target often refer to the customer experience as the target that drives accountability in the stores. This way, as an employee, you understand what you need to do to work toward the Destination of delivering on the ideal Target customer experience. Target has installed red phones throughout the store, and a customer who picks up the receiver will be greeted by a Target team member, more than happy to help find an item in the store or assist in any way.

At the same time, Target has been acutely aware of its external environment. It has stayed ahead of the curve, as upscale consumers embrace casual attire and less affluent shoppers demand more for their money in the absence of bottom-drawer prices. The company developed a stable of exclusive brands, which it sells at a discount, from designer housewares to trendy youth apparel. Although changing demographics pose an ongoing challenge, as Target strives to broaden its Midwestern roots and appeal to an increasingly diverse nation, we have no doubt its adaptability skills bode well for its continued success.

Only time will tell how the saga will play out. We have the highest hopes that these retail industry icons will continue to adapt and, in the process, stay ahead of the game and create new paradigms by not hanging on to the old ones!

[8] THE HUMAN SIDE

Focusing on the Enduring Thing

The time for change is now. In your organization, in your teams, and with the individuals who serve your customers. The metamorphosis into an organization that links people with profits does not happen only because of a company's financial ledgers. It happens because of the hearts and minds of your people and the experience you provide for them.

Herbert Fisk Johnson, Sr., son of SC Johnson founder Samuel Curtis Johnson, Sr., offered an insightful perspective years ago that still holds true today: "The goodwill of the people is the only enduring thing in business," he said in a 1927 Profit-Sharing Day speech. "It is the sole substance. . . . The rest is shadow!"

Every year, 700,000 new businesses are launched—about 80 or so every hour. Plenty are selling the same products and services that your organization sells and would love to have your customers spending money with them. As new competitors emerge, economic conditions shift, and change appears at every turn, what is the enduring thing in your business? What are the sustaining elements that will stabilize your organization during turbulent times as well as increase its success in smoother times?

We believe any organization—large, small, public, private, start-up, mature—can harness the goodwill of its people so that it results in optimal growth for the business. The organizations we've highlighted in this book are astounding evidence of just that. Competitors can copy your products and often offer lower prices, but they will be hard-pressed to win against your people— people who are aware of your Destination, aligned with and accountable for reaching it, and adapting constantly to accelerate business growth and anticipate, embrace, and integrate change long before they must.

Leaders, in turn, must devote themselves to committing time, energy, and focus to the People = Profits ideal. As a leader, every day, you're setting the strategic direction of your organization, but you're also creating the substance of your culture—the very foundation by which everything else is so closely linked. The extent to which you model desired values and behaviors provides the leading example your people will follow—and ultimately win with.

Credibility in Being Human

Trust is a fragile commodity in the world of business because it's hard to earn and easy to lose, especially with your employees. Credibility is one of the most significant parts of building trust and creating followers. It's built over time, by doing what you say you're going to do and by informing others promptly when you can't do what you said you would.

Great leaders lead by admitting mistakes when they are made, capturing the learning, and moving forward. Leaders communicate any deviation or change in expressed values, promises, or Destinations as quickly and as often as possible so that no one is left behind. We encourage all leaders to collect feedback on their perceived credibility by asking others how well they're doing on it. And, of course, by being real. Admitting to another when the trust is low in your relationship is the first, yet critical, step toward rebuilding trust.

> *"What you say you believe in has to be genuine."*
> —Terri Kelly, CEO, W. L. Gore & Associates, Inc.

The leadership at W. L. Gore & Associates understands this fundamental principle: "What you say you believe in has to be genuine. It has to be ingrained in your leaders and the values of everyone inside the organization," says CEO Terri Kelly. "Because if it isn't, everyone will see right through it, and, ultimately, you will fail."

Know your people, and let them know you, too. It's important to tell every person on your leadership team where he or she stands with you and invite the same in return. Your response, even in the face of initiatives that might appear to be failures, will serve to demonstrate the larger vision and values—and prove to your people that you are deeply sincere in your commitment to every Destination.

Information Isn't Communication

There has never been a greater need to get reliable data flowing between individuals and departments within organizations. Yet, despite all the new and innovative ways of communication we have—PDAs, cell phones, e-mail, voice mail—why, in nearly every organization, do employees still rank more effective communication as one of their most serious needs? Is the answer really more communications?

Who really wants to get more e-mail or voice mail? Workplaces have no shortage of information flowing through them each day. What's missing, though, is meaningful communication—back-and-forth exchanges that open dialogue, engage people, and help them connect to the business. Many senior leaders send out e-mails with the best of intentions; but, the message arrives with about 20 others, plus new voice mails, gets prioritized with all the activities of the week, and may never even get read. The e-mail message just couldn't be integrated into the list of things demanding attention on that day.

Communication involves not only transmitting the message but also preparing the message so that listeners have the best chance of hearing it and absorbing it into their understanding. Communication also requires you to be an active listener when others respond to you. Most of us say things in a way that works for us, as the speaker; however, we need to frame things in such a way that our listeners can hear us most effectively.

We're still amazed at the number of misinterpreted e-mails. Because you can't see expressions or hear tone of voice, humor is sometimes taken the wrong way. When someone responds using all capital letters, the recipient might feel like the sender is YELLING BACK. This isn't even information sharing, much less communication. Each time you send a message, test it out from the receiver's perspective. Ask yourself, "Is this the most effective way to have them actually hear what I'm saying?"

Once you send off your message, you'll need to go into listening mode immediately so that the recipient of your message has a chance to respond. This is the way information becomes communication. No one likes to be talked at, but everyone loves to be talked with. True communication also involves choosing the best forum for connecting—from e-mails to phone calls, face-to-face exchanges to town hall meetings—and then listening intentionally.

In school, most of us were trained in the three R's—reading, 'riting, and 'rithmetic—but not in the big L, listening. We were trained to give speeches and to debate but not to listen in return. Yet, more than half of the communication process is listening. Listening with intent to understand will give you insight into people's ideas and opinions that you might not otherwise get. It also makes others feel special and valued and, ultimately, enhances their commitment.

Let's say two people are up for the same job. One gets it, and the manager informs both employees of the decision. That's information. Communication happens when the manager sits down with each employee, explains the decision, and invites feedback: "Robin, here's why you got the job. Here are the expectations." "Duncan, here's why you didn't get the job. Here's what we can do to help you be ready for the job the next time it opens up." Information alone creates questions that each person's mind answers differently, and, many times, incorrectly. Communication ensures that the information is received as it was intended.

The same principles hold true for performance reviews. A once-a-year performance review often does more damage than good. Regular coaching sessions are much more productive and useful for the person receiving the data. They also take away from the pressure to get everything done in a meeting of an hour or two once a year and illustrate the clear difference between information and communication. In frequent, regular meetings, every person has an opportunity to look at his or her contribution over the preceding time period and pinpoint specific goals for maximizing contributions in the future.

*"Today, the only way to stay nimble is to have
dynamic leadership, skillful at communicating to
your employees what you're trying to do and giving them
a vested interest in the success of the company."*

—Joni Reich, Senior Vice President of Administration, Sallie Mae

When an organization is going through a change, leaders may disseminate information—announce that the change is happening—but fail to really communicate the rationale, background, and thought processes behind their decisions. In turn, people don't understand the benefits of accomplishing the organization's chosen Destination. Failure to communicate information about changes results in conflicting or inconsistent messages.

> >> *Is your organization skilled at communicating, or does it mostly inform?*

The Filling-in-the-Blanks Problem

Make sure your managers have all the information they need. When managers don't have the necessary information to pass on to their employees, they often fill in the blanks with what they believe to be true. This is a natural part of being a mid-manager yet is also something that can be costly for an organization. Why? Because managers need to be in the know. They would rather risk sharing information that they believe to be true than admit that they don't know or haven't been told by senior leaders.

Every one of us wants to be viewed as competent. And most of us will do what we need to do to feel that we are. The problem with managers filling in the blanks is that the real information is lost as rumors and speculation take over. Eventually, being in the dark leads to disengagement and diminished productivity, regardless of where you are in the organization. The most effective communication, then, is geared toward connecting rather than informing.

East Alabama Medical Center makes a distinct effort to communicate new initiatives. When EAMC started a program to reduce health care costs for its employees, putting more pressure on people to take responsibility for their health, the program was accompanied by "massive communication," says HR Director Susan Johnston. "We're getting into their business a little bit. That's a change in culture for us. We don't want anything to be a surprise to our people."

EAMC also demonstrates its devotion to employee communications with a biannual Employee Satisfaction Survey. Employees provide feedback and then receive survey results along with a further opportunity to express their opinions at ongoing meetings facilitated by EAMC leaders. Managers are required to submit action plans for addressing any issue that surfaces from the survey, and these results are again communicated to employees.

Alston & Bird uses town meetings as a way of communicating with employees. The firm continues to grow through mergers, and leaders realize that it takes time for people to get comfortable with one another. After a merger, leaders go on the road and hold town meetings where they answer all questions from employees. Instead of conducting employee surveys, the firm prefers to bring people together in small focus groups that create an environment of openness and candor. Policies are tweaked only after listening to what employees have to say in these small-group settings.

>> *Do you encourage open dialogue that actively engages people?*

Wisdom Moving Upward

In linking people to the organization, effective communication is a continuous three-way process: getting the word out, spreading the word within, and bringing the wisdom up.

Studies have found that the higher up a person is in the organization, the less he or she knows about what's really going on inside the organization. On the one hand, executives typically are aware of only 5 percent of the issues of concern inside their organization because they need to have an external focus. On the other hand, employees at the lowest level of the organization are 100 percent aware of internal issues because they live them each day, yet they may be unaware of the organization's external concerns. A two-way communication flow throughout the organization is ideal. Employees at the lower levels need to have access to the upper levels so they can share their wisdom on what's really happening inside. Those at the top need to educate on what's happening outside and push it through the organization so that employees make the best decisions.

The ability to communicate is a challenge that can be overcome by simply taking the time, at every single meeting, to consider who might benefit from knowing the information and then ensuring that the information is shared quickly and thoroughly. The goal is to establish this as a routine and consistent practice.

>> *How do you teach people to listen at your organization?*

The 100-100 Rule

Each time you send a message, test it out from the receiver's perspective. Ask yourself, "Is this the most effective way to have them actually hear what I'm saying?"

For every communication you have, we suggest you adopt the 100-100 Rule. A 50-50, sender-receiver model for effective communication is often touted. You say something, and then I say something. But when both parties meet each other halfway, it will most likely produce half the results.

We believe the only model that works in every part of the 4-A Process is the 100-100 Rule. The 100-100 Rule suggests that when you communicate with others, you're 100 percent responsible for ensuring that what you're saying is fully understood by your audience—from your boss, to your team, to your customers, to your family members. The responsibility rests with you, always. You need to be sure that the other person gets it before the conversation is done.

Similarly, when others are speaking or communicating with you, the ownership of understanding is 100 percent yours. Take responsibility for ensuring that you're getting what they're telling you. Typically, you can do this through active listening by paraphrasing what you have heard. We like the phrase "Let me play back what I heard so I'm sure I got it."

To recap, when you speak to others, you own 100 percent of the responsibility to ensure that they get it. When others speak to you, you own 100 percent of the responsibility to ensure that you get it. Welcome to the profitable world of communication!

Why People Stay, Not Why They Leave

It's much better to have people quit and leave—than quit and stay! When an employee leaves an organization, leaders tend to ask, "Why are you leaving?" What they don't do enough of is to ask their top talent, "Why are you staying?" It's important to know why your top contributors have been able to be top contributors because you can then work toward replicating that experience for more of your workforce.

Knowing why some of your people are superstars is much more valuable than knowing why some people are low performers. While it seems to make sense to resolve the problems of lower performers, doing so can detract from those employees who make you the most money. We're not suggesting that you forget about low performers. However, if your organization is like most others, your managers are solving the wrong problems. You're trying to fix what's wrong instead of building on what's already right.

When leaders focus on low performers, top talent is often ignored. If your organization doesn't acknowledge and reinforce the contributions of your top talent, they may lose their passion to shine. It's not that they need the recognition as much as it is that they love to get things done. The worst thing to do is to hire top performers and bring them into an inefficient organization or one that blocks their progress toward a Destination. Low performers, in contrast, thrive on inefficiency, because that's how they keep their jobs!

How many people at your company are powerhouses of knowledge and innovative ideas but are not being fully leveraged—or maybe not even being allowed—to use all they have? Hiring great people but not allowing their perspectives to become part of the culture stifles their commitment and your organization's productivity.

>> *Who is your top talent? What are you doing right to help them deliver on their potential? How can you duplicate the experience they're having and spread it throughout your organization?*

Often, the inability to encourage top talent to execute, regardless of rank, is driven by fear. Leaders may feel that they need to keep their workforce under control, which is a huge waste of a major investment in people, usually one of the most significant costs any organization has.

Study the best in your organization. Listen for what they talk about; understand the issues they raise; understand why they do what they do. Learn how they balance their needs against the needs of the organization. Apply what you find toward integrating your systems of hiring, retention, and people development.

Along with top talent, all organizations have top influencers—those people who, regardless of rank, are well liked and can easily influence others to get things done. Influencers often are in support roles because they have regular access to everyone on the team. They are key allies with a subtle power to move your organization to greater profit and productivity. Creating special meetings for them and soliciting their suggestions periodically can deepen awareness of your organization's progress toward its Destinations, alert you to issues to address before they become urgent, and help you get things accomplished through the informal networks embedded in your organization, as in every organization in existence today.

> > *Who are the biggest influencers in your organization?*

Fun, Fun, Fun

Organizations that are successful in connecting people to the business really know how to have fun. In many workplaces, like W. L. Gore, fun is as important as profit. "Humor," says Bob Doak of Gore "is a kind of humility. We're only human. And what binds us all together is that none of us is perfect. We're here to help one another and, ultimately, we're going to make money, and have fun doing it."

A major source of fun at Gore is the company's robust volleyball league. The league has three divisions, and the games are a favorite activity, taking place twice a week in the summer. After sitting in on some of them, we saw that Gore associates can be just as competitive in their volleyball games as they are in their business—and still have some serious fun!

"You've got to have humor at work."
—Bob Doak, W. L. Gore & Associates, Inc.

It may seem unusual for laughter to be a core value in a health care setting, but humor is essential at East Alabama Medical Center. While not making light of the critical work they do each day, the people of EAMC like to laugh and have a good time. In an effort to get employees enthused about a visit from the Joint Commission, the accrediting body for health organizations, the center launched a *Wheel of Fortune* event. CEO Terry Andrus dressed up as show hostess Vanna White. "He walked through our entire organization, quizzing employees on likely questions from the Joint Commission," says HR Director Susan Johnston. Not only was it entertaining, but how could they forget the answers after seeing Terry in an evening gown?

Then there was the time EAMC issued its biannual Employee Satisfaction Survey. "We said Terry would kiss a pig if we got at least 75 percent participation," Johnston relates. "We got 88 percent participation. Needless to say, a lot of pig-kissing went on that day."

Perkins Coie has raised social events to an art form. Along with ice cream socials and excursions to Seattle Mariners baseball games, the firm hosts a huge holiday party every December. It assigns its newest attorneys to a skit committee, or, in Perkins Coie parlance, Skitcom. "The goal is to outdo the previous year," explains Chief Personnel Officer Darrin Emerick. "It's always a parody of a current event happening at the firm, in the U.S., or around the world." One of the most memorable skits was a take-off on a company event, showcasing a change in flu shot providers.

"People had to wait in line 25 minutes to get their shots," Emerick says. "It was a fiasco." So that year, the skit featured an attorney dressed as a nurse, doling out flu shots with a caulk gun.

Southwest is legendary for encouraging its people to enjoy their jobs. In hiring, the company looks for a sense of humor because fun and laughter are essential parts of its culture. Typical interview questions may include "Give me an example of how you've used your sense of humor in a work environment" or "Tell me how you've used humor to defuse a tense situation."

On the job, employees are encouraged to have fun with their customers. One morning, a flight attendant announced over the speaker, "Welcome aboard, everyone. We need to acknowledge that we have a very important person on board this morning. It's his birthday today, and he's turning 103. This is the first time he's ever flown!"

The aisles were abuzz with speculation, as everyone looked around the plane to see who looked 103. When the flight attendant got back on the speaker, she said, "OK, folks, on your way out, be sure to wish our captain a happy birthday!" Immediately following the roar of laughter, strangers began talking and getting to know one another. Such relationships result in continued loyalty to the airline. In fact, to date, more than 300 couples have been married on a Southwest plane! It truly is the airline of LUV (Southwest's symbol on the New York Stock Exchange).

These fun exchanges not only make the employee's work more enjoyable but illustrate how Southwest has built fun into its business model in order to advance its Destination: creating an enjoyable flying experience. This Destination puts the company miles ahead of traditional legacy carriers.

JetBlue Airways builds fun into the employee and customer experience at every touchpoint. If you've ever noticed a JetBlue airplane tail, it's easy to feel that the manufacturer of these planes has a lighthearted touch. Tails come in seven different styles: striped, harlequin, dots and squares, windowpane, bubbles, tartan, and mosaic. Employees are invited to name the planes. In fact, every JetBlue airplane has been named by an employee, and each name incorporates the word Blue. The creative christenings are guaranteed to bring a smile: Blue Flight Special, Hopelessly Devoted to Blue, Bada Bing Bada Blue, You and Me and a Jet Named Blue.

When a new plane is ordered, employees write in suggesting names and explaining the reasons behind their choices. If your name is chosen, you and your family and friends get to fly to France or Brazil to pick up the aircraft and then fly home in it. You get to be in the airplane as it rolls off the line. It's a simple investment, but it's created a tremendous connection to the business.

> > *What and how does your organization celebrate and have fun?*

Power for Giving Away

Don't hoard your power. Give it away to others. Great leaders have always known this! Share your knowledge, techniques, and experiences freely. A manager needs credit, but a leader gives credit to others. The 4-A Process is designed to build leaders who freely give away their power.

Involve employees in any process that affects them. Engage them in setting Destinations. People want to be proud of their work and their organizations. Ask for their buy-in. Give them the ability to run with their ideas. Ensure that they have the right skills and resources to deliver on the Destinations.

Listen to what people are saying—and what they're not saying but may be signaling. Push information out instead of constraining or controlling it. Constrained organizations ultimately choke themselves.

Communicate, communicate, communicate! Let people know where they're going and involve them every step of the way. Make the new employment contract one of shared purpose. Empowerment is best used when people are united in a common goal and are doing what they do best to move the organization toward that goal. In the end, people will want to be aligned to reach the Destination, and held accountable for doing so, because they'll know "we're all in this together."

These are the high-level lessons we've learned from the organizations profiled in this book. On the next two pages, we offer 10 tips for putting these lessons to work. We call them "carry-ons," as they will help you carry on from where you are today to where you want to be tomorrow in your journey to becoming an adaptable, people-centric, and profitable paradigm breaker!

What's Really Important

As we come to the end of this book, we'd like to share a story about Profit-Sharing Day at SC Johnson. It's an event that celebrates the power, promise, and connection of the company's 12,000 employees, on a special day when people share in what's really important to them. The experience is one that reflects the message of this book—connecting people to your business.

In this celebration, held every year in December, everyone gathers together at company headquarters in Racine, Wisconsin, or links in through satellite hookup at the company's locations throughout the world. Profit-Sharing Day has become a legacy of every SC Johnson employee worldwide. However, the profit-sharing checks are just a small part of this remarkable day, the best day of the year for many SCJ employees.

Carry-Ons

1. **See things differently.** Think like a start-up. Look at industry data, trends, and events from a fresh perspective. It's like they say, if you keep on doing what you've been doing, you'll keep on getting what you've already got!

2. **Use real and timely data.** Your ability to adapt is only as good as the data you have. Set your Destinations and base your decisions on the latest information. Ensure that each Destination you set is designed to increase cash flow.

3. **Study where you've gone before.** Look at your previous Destinations —what worked and what didn't—from the organizational, team, and individual perspectives. Your organization is an underused yet powerful place for benchmarking the past and forecasting the future.

4. **Be externally informed and internally driven.** Build the infrastructure that channels information rapidly, for results you can act on immediately. Any lag time is a missed opportunity and could give the competition a chance to take away your future.

5. **Align your leadership team.** The more successful you are at gaining the support of your executive team, the faster you'll connect people with profit. Express your Destination and demonstrate your dedication in such a way that your leaders share it with exuberance and can help everyone in your organization experience it with the same intensity.

6. **Create more market space as opposed to seeking more market share.** Stop trying to take business from your competitors; it's business that's already there. Instead, create new markets for your products and services. We call this the "Southwest Effect." When Southwest goes into new markets, instead of taking fliers away from other carriers, it creates additional demand for its flights and finds new channels to sell.

7. Be intentional, and keep it simple. Use the "chunking" method we describe throughout the book to reach your Destinations. Whenever it starts to get complicated, take the most direct and least resistant route.

8. Take it one interaction at a time. Your ideal culture of excellence is based on beliefs and values, but it's expressed through behaviors, one interaction at a time. These interactions combined make a culture and propel your people forward.

9. Create your own path. Remember that there is no cookie-cutter, one-size-fits-all culture. Build the culture that's just right for you, leveraging your Optimum People Profit Opportunities, your "thing," and the unique contributions of every human being.

10. Make sure your people have the resources to deliver. Linking people with profits is an exercise in equipping your people with the knowledge, skills, and technology to do what you've asked them to do. Instead of fixing your organization into greatness, build greatness into your organization by finding what's right and doing more of it.

It's the only day at SCJ that's not "business casual." Everyone dresses up out of respect for the tradition and the event, which has been going on since 1917. As part of the tradition, SCJ employees have morning beverages, complete with Kringles, a pastry made in Racine. Mid-morning, they grab any remaining Kringles for the road, eagerly head toward the line-up of yellow buses, and then they jump aboard for a spirited ride to gather with their colleagues.

The buses and cars pull up to a building that houses a huge gymnasium. SC Johnson employees hop out and gather inside the gym. They are there to celebrate and to connect—to the

Johnson family, to the business, and, most important, to one another. Holiday lights surround them. People hug, laugh, and hand out candy canes and other tokens of the season. It's noisy. It's energized. In many ways, it feels like a huge family reunion—with 2,500 people!

Then, the start of the official program is announced. People scramble to find seats as the room quiets down. They wave across the aisles to friends and co-workers, while, at center stage, a Johnson family member welcomes them to another Profit-Sharing Day celebration. The crowd goes nuts. Seated in the front row of this enormous room is the Johnson family, from patriarchs and matriarchs to a flock of grandchildren. They rise and give updates on their families. After all, SC Johnson is a family company.

The day is capped with a festive party, paid for personally by the chairman and CEO, Fisk Johnson. It extends throughout the day and is filled with celebrations of everyone's hard work during the past year. Then, after everyone has mingled, eaten, and fully enjoyed the day, the employees receive their profit-sharing checks from a member of the leadership team.

After Profit-Sharing Day is over, the company shuts down, sometimes for up to two weeks, as an additional thank-you to employees. This happens all over the world, in more than 110 SCJ offices. The celebrations vary from country to country but are always focused on giving back to employees for their many contributions throughout the year.

Sam Johnson, a legend at SCJ for both his leadership and his humanity, attended his last Profit-Sharing Day in December 2003. This was a difficult time for Sam, as he was fighting a fierce battle with pancreatic cancer. He was hospitalized near the end of the year, and it looked as if he would miss Profit-Sharing Day. His doctors and family didn't think he should leave the hospital. Sam, however, thought differently. He realized the importance of coming home that year—to his family, his employees, and, most important, himself. Sam must have known this was the last time he would attend this special event. "I'm coming home," he said.

And come home he did. Sam's message that day was short, but one that will shine forever in the memories of those who watched him make his way, haltingly, to the podium—realizing with his every step the power of the human spirit. Sam shared his absolute certainty that Profit-Sharing Day was the best day of the year. There was just a certain magic to it that you couldn't find anywhere else. Then he told everyone in the room how much he loved SCJ. How much he loved his wife, kids, and grandkids. And, especially, how much he loved the people of SCJ. Employees say it was the most amazing expression of leadership and caring you could ever get from a leader.

Sam was a powerful businessman. He understood how to both make money and have fun. When he became president of SC Johnson in 1966, at the age of 37, he was the fourth generation of his family to lead the business. Then, the company had annual sales of $171 million; today, Johnson Family Enterprises generates annual sales of more than $6.5 billion. In 1993, President Bill Clinton appointed Sam to the U.S. President's Council on Sustainable Development, a national policy advisory council for the world. He held seven honorary doctoral degrees and received numerous international awards in recognition of his global business, environmental, and philanthropic contributions. He was also inducted into the prestigious U.S. National Business Hall of Fame.

But, beyond his many accomplishments, Sam was humble. Warm. Human. The kind of leader people want to follow. He passed away in May 2004, leaving behind an unwavering love, commitment, and triumphant dedication to "This We Believe." Sam believed. And he got others to believe through his commitment to people and to the humanity of his organization.

Bubble-Blowing with Gracie

On the day of Sam's funeral, the family decided to close the business. Sam's son Fisk, now SCJ's chairman and CEO, said that family members had wanted employees to feel they could take the day to do what was always so important to Sam: spend time with the family.

Kelly Semrau, vice president of global public affairs and communication, vividly recalls the day as one she will never forget. Kelly attended Sam's memorial service with her team, and, afterward, returned home to her family, where she taught her 15-month-old daughter Gracie how to blow bubbles.

For Kelly, this was her tribute to a great leader: teaching Gracie how to blow bubbles while she and her husband enjoyed a peaceful moment in the backyard, talking about Sam and reflecting on him as a leader and a person.

"As a top female exec, that I have the ability to be so 'mushy gushy' is a powerful expression of who SCJ is as a company," Kelly reflects. "It is one of the greatest rewards I have ever received. More than taking on important projects. More than becoming a company officer. Just having this day to connect with my family, as Sam connected with his family of employees, was an amazing gift. This is something you just don't get every day."

Organizations that are winning are living the power of this type of connection, every hour of every day. Creating meaning with, for, and through their people. Embracing the power of the human spirit by connecting people to business is an approach that serves everyone. It is what founder Samuel Curtis Johnson, his son, H. F. Johnson, Sr., and their remarkable family have known all along: People are the sole substance of any organization. The rest is shadow.

INDEX

Accountability: adaptability gained through, 180; admitting of mistakes and, 165; commitments and, 163; connected culture and, 168–170; constructive feedback and, 172–173; contribution-oriented culture, 171–172; definition of, 161; elements of, 162; excuses vs., 163–164; focus of, 99; high-performance team building, 102–103; individual application of, 103; manager's role in, 175–178; maximizing of, 175–178; meetings and, 174–175; organization application of, 101; performance and, 165; pressure to perform and, 165–167; progress assessments and, 167; self-responsibility and, 164; Southwest Airlines case study of, 101

adaptability, 179
adaptable leaders, 200
Adaptation: benefits of, 182–183; change management vs., 184; description of, 181–182; development of, 187; endless cycle of, 183–184; feedback as part of, 195–196; focus of, 100; Ford Motors example of, 194–195; goal of, 187; high-performance team building, 103; individual application of, 103; methods of, 187; as mind-set, 182; need for, 107; 9/11 as example of, 185; organization application of, 101; principles of, 184; signals regarding the need for, 194–195; Southwest Airlines example of, 101, 187–188

adaptation, 95–97
advancement, 16
advances: description of, 16; example of, 17
Ahlrichs, Nancy, 2
aligned organizations, 140, 147–148, 153–157, 160
Alignment: achieving of, 151–153; benefits of, 160; customer service as indicator of, 139–140; focus of, 99; high-performance team building, 102; individual application of, 103; for individuals, 149–151; leadership's role in, 157–159; organization application of, 101; processes involved in, 140; shared mind-set for, 143–146; Southwest Airlines case study of, 101; team, 146–148, 226
Alston & Bird, 23, 31, 60, 66, 70, 82, 178, 195, 217
Amazon.com, 148
Andrus, Terry, 27–28, 75, 84, 156, 157, 222
attainable goals, 35
auditory learners, 176
Awareness: focus of, 99, 113–114; high-performance team building, 102; individual application of, 103; organization application of, 101; purpose of, 111–112; of route options and diversions, 123; Southwest Airlines case study of, 101

Baity, Gail, 30, 94, 126, 140
Barger, David, 12, 125–126
Barger, Mike, 12, 45, 58, 67, 81, 96, 125–126, 150, 154, 185, 191, 197
Benton, Cathy, 23, 31, 60, 66, 70, 178, 195
Bethlehem Steel, 189
Bethune, Gordon, 124–125
Bezos, Jeff, 148
blaming, 163–164, 193
Bonner, Robert, 29, 115–116
Bright Grey, 86–87
building, 17

Bush, George W., 115
business: connecting of people to, 43–66, 197; new hire's understanding of, 55; people and, 2–6
business practices, 53
business relationships: with colleagues, 48–49; with company, 46–47; with customers, 51–53; with job, 49–50; overview of, 46; with supervisor, 47–48

career, 50–51
Causey, Jean, 28
Central Express, 57–58
Chambers, Jeff, 6, 25, 80, 81, 83, 84, 98, 119, 187
change: accommodating to, 91; adapting to, 95–97; blame for, 193; communicating of, 216; denial of, 193; in Destinations, 19–20; 4-A process view of, 107–108; involvement in, 92; large-scale, 108; need for, 109; prevalence of, 89; problem solving for, 193–194; reactions to, 90–92, 192–194; rejection of, 193; resistance to, 95–96, 109; surprise at, 192–193; thinking process used for, 109; time for, 211; traditional models of, 106–107
change management, 184
channels of input, 118–120
"chunking" of destinations, 37–39, 120, 227
coaching sessions, 215
Coca-Cola, 56, 136
colleagues, 48–49
commitment, 72–77, 162–163
communication: in aligned organization, 153; of change, 216; for connecting, 216–217; effectiveness of, 218; elements of, 214–215; lack of, 213–214; between leaders and employees, 218; leader's influence on, 11; listening involved in, 214; methods of, 215; need for, 214; 100-100 rule, 218–219

companies: connecting of people to, 46–47; financial information shared with employees, 21–24; interdepartmental competition, 147; values of, 14–16, 60. *See also* organization(s)
competency, 216–217
competition: description of, 1; prevalence of, 51–52; watching of, 159–160
complacency, 94
connected culture, 32, 168–170
connected people: benefits of, 8; case example of, 8–9; change and, 192; monetary savings from, 24–25; after 9/11, 33–34
connecting of employees: in aligned organizations, 153; beginning of, 56; to business, 43–66, 197; business performance and, 34; to company, 46–47; Destination and, 35–43; information used for, 216–217; ongoing nature of, 45–46; opportunities for, 34, 45; perks and benefits used for, 39–40; profit benefits from, 61; to supervisor, 47–48
consensus-seeking, 145
constrained organizations, 225
constructive feedback, 172–173
Container Store, 71
Continental Airlines, 124–125
Contribution Coaching Model, 172
contribution-oriented culture, 171–172
contribution reviews, 198
Con-way, 8–9, 57, 72, 75, 82, 122, 170, 201
core issues, 41–43
Corning Incorporated, 30–31, 71, 93–94
credibility, 212–213
cross-training, 50–51
customers: commitment from, 74; connection with, 51–53, 105; employee connection with, 154; expectations of, 190–191; integrated experiences, 190–191; listening to, 43

customer satisfaction, 120
customer service: Alignment and, 139–140; importance of, 7; negative experiences in, 7; positive experiences in, 7–8

Data Return, 20–21, 40, 46–47, 60, 67, 72, 160, 169
decision making: alignment and, 148; description of, 145; employee knowledge and, 203
dedicated employees, 44
denial of change, 193
Destination(s): aggressive discounting as, 207–208; broad, 119–120; challenges associated with, 40–41; changes in, 19–20; "chunking" of, 37–39, 120, 227; clarity of, 117; connecting people and, 35–43; constraints on, 178–179; core issues for determining, 41–42; evaluation of, 39–41; example of, 119; first to differentiate as, 136; first to market as, 135–138; focus on, 35–36, 137; goals vs., 112; imperatives for, 19; individual focus of, 127; irrelevant, 114; job alignment with, 151; at Kmart, 205–207; knowledge of, 116–117; metrics for, 137; milestones in achieving, 137; moving merchandise quickly as, 205–207; multiple, 35–36, 100, 112; number of, 35–36; organizational, 100–101, 115–117; organizational culture used to achieve, 130–135; profit as, 61; purpose of, 100, 112; pursuing of, 122–123; realistic type of, 37–38, 129–130; reinforcing of, 130; start, stop, and continue strategy, 126; strengths-based approach to, 122; style as, 208–209; at Target, 208–209; for teams, 126–127; tips for, 137–138; transparency about, 138; vague, 114, 119–120; visualizing of, 20; at Wal-Mart, 207–208

Destination Analysis, 178–180
Destination Champion, 118, 151–153
Destination Planning: description of, 112; employees' participation in, 128–129; organization focus, 124–126; team focus, 126–127
development plans, 202
disconnecting of employees, 15–16, 45, 176–177
division of focus, 105
division-of-labor focus, 105, 189
Doak, Bob, 3, 120, 221–222
Donnell, Jim, 76
Dornan, John, 71, 165
dude theory, 82

East Alabama Medical Center, 23, 27–28, 49, 74, 84, 130, 156, 157, 191, 217, 222
e-mail, 214
Emerick, Darrin, 27, 222–223
employees: in achieving Destination, 117; as associates, 198; career promotion for, 50–51; celebrating the accomplishments of, 59–60; change reactions, 192–194; charitable opportunities for, 61–62; commitment by, 74, 162; common interests among, 64–66; company savings by connecting with, 24–25; connecting of. See connecting of employees; connective experience for, 7–8; control of, 220; customer connections, 52; dedicated, 44; descriptive terms for, 197–199; Destination Planning participation by, 128–129; disconnecting of, 15–16, 45, 176–177; disengaged, 10; empowerment of, 5–6, 162; engagement in processes, 224; equitable experience for, 77–82; external environment understood by, 203; fairness among, 78–82; financial information of

company shared with, 21–24; fun for, 221–224; hierarchy of, 82; hiring of, 69–72, 149–150, 220; influential types of, 221; input by, 118–120; knowledge of, 203–204; laying off of, 15, 93–94; leader accessibility to, 13–14; leadership needs of, 48; learning style of, 176; leveraging the abilities of, 177–178; listening to, 193–194; low-performing, 220; meaning at work for, 29–30; monetary savings by investing in, 24–25; motivation of, 30–31, 64, 168–170; needs of, 203–204; not-so-dedicated, 44–45; onboarding of, 53–59; patience of, 71; personal profile of, 175–176; power of, 32; profile of, 9–10; quitting by, 219–220; recognition for, 44, 59–60, 170; relationship building by, 37; resiliency of, 138; resources for, 227; rewards for, 170; selfless acts by, 62; shared mind-set among, 143–146; status differences among, 82; top talent in, 69–70; training of, 26, 71; types of, 44; unhappy, 10; value of, 30; "you're lucky to work here" mentality for, 15. See also people
employee turnover, 141
empowerment: description of, 162; in organizational culture, 5–6; use of, 225
excuses, 163–164

fairness, 77–82
family-work balance, 26–27
Federal Express, 156
feedback: Accountability and, 172–173; Adaptation and, 196; collecting of, 195–197, 213
Ferraro, Karen, 133
financial information: employee's knowledge of, 21–24
fixing, 17

focus: of Accountability, 99; of Adaptation, 100; of Alignment, 99; of Awareness, 99, 113–114; division of, 105; division-of-labor, 105, 189; in organizations, 113
focused management approach, 167
followership, 77
Ford Motors, 194–195
4-A process: change as viewed by, 106–107; factors that affect, 108; for individuals, 103, 105; levels of effectiveness, 100–108; 100-100 rule, 219; for organizations, 101–102, 104; overview of, 98–100; schematic diagram of, 99; sequence of, 108; for teams, 102–103; variations in, 107–108. *See also* Accountability; Adaptation; Alignment; Awareness
fun, 221–224

goals: attainability of, 35; Destinations vs., 112
Goodnight, Jim, 5, 13, 25, 119
Guiding Principles, 46–47, 60, 76

Herwald, Kurt, 188
high-performance teams, 102
hiring of employees, 69–72, 149–150, 220
Honda, 194
human doings, 26–29

incompetence, 96
individuals: alignment for, 149–151; Destination focus on, 127; 4-A process applied to, 103, 105, 106; hiring of, 149–150; value descriptions for, 150–151
influencers, 221
information: as power, 18; for managers, 216–217
Instant Coaching, 173
integrated customer experiences, 190–191
interactions in organizations, 32
internship programs, 50–51

Jannausch, Pat, 8, 9, 57, 170, 201
JetBlue Airways, 12–13, 58–59, 67, 81–82, 86, 96, 125, 150, 154–156, 184, 185–186, 191, 196–197, 203, 223–224
job: business relationship with, 49–50; flexibility of, 49; onboarding of employees, 53–59
job descriptions, 150–151
Johnson, Ben, 32
Johnson, H. F. Sr., 211, 230
Johnson, Sam, 228–230
Johnston, Susan, 191, 217, 222

Kelleher, Herb, 102, 188
Kelly, Terri, 3, 76–77, 145, 157, 177–178, 213
Kenlon, Anne, 70, 182
kinesthetic learners, 176
Kmart, 91, 159–160, 205–207

Land's End, 51
language, 197–199
leaders: accessibility of, 11–14; adaptable, 200; change for, 11; company examples of, 13; employee accessibility to, 13–14; feedback collected by, 213; focus on low performers, 220; followers of, 158; giving away power by, 224–225; inspiration by, 77; mistakes by, 213; open communication promoted by, 11; traits of, 111
leadership: Alignment facilitated by, 157–159; creation of, 157; traits necessary for, 158
learning, 109
learning styles, 176
legacy, 68
leveraging the abilities of employees, 177–178
listening: communication and, 214–215; to employees, 193–194; importance of, 215; intensive, 195–197

management theories, 189
managers: employee-related information needed by, 175–178; information for, 216–217; maximizing accountability, 175–178
market space, 226
McDonald's, 122, 141–142
McGowan, Bill, 91
Medtronic, 62
meetings, 174–175, 215, 217
mind-set: Adaptation as, 182; shared, 143–146
misaligned organizations, 36, 141–143
mistakes, 165, 213
motivation, 64, 168–170

needs-first, solutions-second approach, 43
Neeleman, David, 12, 125–126
Newcor Steel, 189
new hires: basics for, 53–54; onboarding of, 53–59; orientation programs for, 57; rules, roles, and resources of organization, 55; understanding of business by, 55
9/11, 33–34, 185
not-so-dedicated employees, 44–45

onboarding, 53–59
100-100 rule, 218–219
operating beliefs, 131
Optimum People-Profit Opportunities: description of, 121–122, 141; hiring for, 149
Oracle, 119
organization(s): adaptation to change, 95–97; aligned, 140, 147–148, 153–157, 160; business practices of, 53; channels of input in, 118–120; commitment fostered by, 162; connecting of people to, 46–47; constrained, 224–225; customer connections with, 105; describing of, 73; doing what's working for you, 202; externally informed and internally driven, 199–200, 226; fairness in, 78–82; financial information shared with employees, 21–24; focus in, 113; 4-A process applied to, 101–102, 104; fragmentation in, 188–190; goals of, 126; influencers in, 129, 221; interactions in, 32; irrelevant, 113–114; language used in, 197–199; misaligned, 36, 141–143; past business models used by, 105; policies of, 74–75, 80; power in, 72, 74; profit-driven, 61; recognition within, 127–128, 170; reinventing of, 89, 94–95, 189–190; relevancy of, 113–114; rules, roles, and resources of, 55; start-up, 107–108, 189, 211–212; training programs, 50, 71; trend following by, 200–201; trust building by, 83–85
organizational culture: blaming in, 163–164; building of, 67, 227; characteristics of, 67; connected, 32, 168–170; contribution-oriented, 171–172; defining of, 66–68; descriptions associated with, 69; Destination achievement by using, 130–135; empowerment of people in, 5–6; examples of, 69–72; importance of, 3–4; misfits with, 168; openness in, 4; performance-based, 163; refocusing of, 165; top talent as viewed through, 69–70; trust in, 83–85
organizational Destinations: description of, 112, 115–117; individuals' behaviors and responsibilities, 120; Optimum People-Profit Opportunities, 121–122; Southwest Airlines case study of, 124; for teams, 126–127
orientation programs, 57

patience, 71
peer support, 177
people: business and, 2–6; change reactions, 192–194; connected. *See* connected people; empowerment of, 5–6, 162; goodwill of, 211; human side of, 63–66; importance of, 1–2; learning style of, 176; motivation for, 64, 168–170; needs of, 64; power of, 32; profits linked with, 227; resiliency of, 138; resources for, 227. *See also* employees
People Express, 185–186
performance: accountability and, 165; feelings and, 63–64; maximizing of, 91; new hire's understanding of, 55–56; organizational culture built around, 163; pressure related to, 165–166
performance reviews, 171–172, 198, 202, 215
Perkins Coie, 27, 63, 66, 222–223
perks, 39–40
personal profile, 175–176
policies, 74–75, 80
positive recognition, 60
power: of employees, 32; giving away of, 224–225; information as, 18; leaders and, 77; in organizations, 72, 74
pressure, 165–167
problem solving: approaches to, 16; for change, 193–194; importance of, 41
profitability, 122
profits: as Destination, 61; organizations driven by, 61; people linked with, 227
progress evaluation: "every eight hours" approach, 167–168; incremental approach to, 171
purpose-driven job, 29–32

quitting, 219–220

recognition of employees, 44, 59–60, 170
Reich, Joni, 11, 24, 46, 49–50, 70, 93, 216
resiliency, 138
retreats, 16
Revlon, 50
rewards, 170
risk-taking, 4
Ritz-Carlton, 169
Robinson, David, 86–87

Sallie Mae, 11–12, 23–24, 46, 49–50, 62–63, 70, 82, 93
SAS Institute, 5–6, 13, 24–26, 39, 71, 80–81, 83–84, 97–98, 119, 135, 187
SC Johnson, 24, 67–68, 75, 122, 133, 136, 146, 150, 174, 211, 225, 227–230
SEI Investments, 133
self-blame, 193
self-responsibility, 164
Semrau, Kelly, 24, 68, 75, 150, 230
Service Quality Indicators, 156
shared mind-set, 143–146
Southwest Airlines, 4–5, 13, 20, 22–23, 38, 60, 74, 101–102, 121, 124, 150, 154, 184, 187–188, 223, 226
Stagen, Rand, 60, 67, 160
stagnant quo, 18, 85–87
stakeholders: Destination achievement told to, 130; needs of, 127
Starbucks, 36–37, 122
start-up organizations, 108, 189, 211–212
Stevens Aviation, 188
supervisor: business relationship with, 47–48; in connecting of people to organization, 47–48; trust of, 47

Target, 159–160, 208–209
task, respect for, 48
TD Industries, 28–29

teams: Alignment of, 146–148, 226; 4-A process applied to, 102–103; high-performance, 102
Timberland, 62
top talent, 69–70, 219–221
Toyota, 159, 194
training of employees, 26, 71
trend following, 200–201
trust: breaking of, 84; building of, 48, 83–85; credibility and, 212–213; description of, 15; fragility of, 212; rebuilding of, 213; restoring of, 84–85; of supervisor, 47

unfairness, 77–78
U.S. Customs and Border Protection, 29–30, 115–116

vague Destinations, 114, 119–120
value: creating of, 183; of employees, 30
value descriptions, 150–151
values: reinforcing of, 60; at work, 30
Vanderbeck, Sunny, 20–21, 40, 46, 72, 169

vision statements, 119
visualizing: of Destination, 20; examples of, 20–21
visual learners, 176
voice mails, 214

Wal-Mart, 156–157, 159, 198, 200, 207–208
Wegmans, 65
Weiss, Robert, 29
Welch, Jack, 2
Whirlpool, 191
W. L. Gore & Associates, 2–4, 18–19, 40–41, 50–51, 75–77, 81, 122, 131–133, 145, 157, 162, 177, 198, 213, 221–222
work: fairness at, 78–81; family balance with, 26–27; meaning in, 29–32; unfairness at, 78
workplace: building of, 38; connection at, 34; fun in, 221–224; incentives in, 59; value at, 30

"you're lucky to work here" mentality, 15